Writer: Ken Vose
Book Design and Lead Photography by: Matthew Eberhart
Senior Associate Design Director: Doug Samuelson
Assistant Art Director: Chad Jewell
Cover Photographer (Jesse James photo): Eric Hameister
Contributing Illustrator: Craig Fraser
Contributing Writers: John P. Holms, Larry Johnston, Jeff Smith
Copy Chief: Terri Fredrickson
Editorial Operations Manager: Karen Schirm
Managers, Book Production: Pam Kvitne,
  Marjorie J. Schenkelberg, Rick von Holdt
Contributing Photo Editor: Joan Luckett
Contributing Story Scout: Ron Mack, Weld Racing
Contributing Proofreaders: David Craft, Beth Havey,
  Sara Henderson, David Krause
Editorial and Design Assistants: Kaye Chabot,
  Patty Loder, Karen McFadden
Edit and Design Production Coordinator: Mary Lee Gavin

Meredith Books
Editor in Chief: Linda Raglan Cunningham
Design Director: Matt Strelecki
Managing Editor: Gregory H. Kayko
Executive Editor: Dan Rosenberg

Publisher: James D. Blume
Executive Director, Marketing: Jeffrey Myers
Executive Director, New Business Development: Todd M. Davis
Executive Director, Sales: Ken Zagor
Director, Operations: George A. Susral
Director, Production: Douglas M. Johnston
Business Director: Jim Leonard

Vice President and General Manager: Douglas J. Guendel

Meredith Publishing Group
President, Publishing Group: Stephen M. Lacy
Vice President-Publishing Director: Bob Mate

Meredith Corporation
Chairman and Chief Executive Officer: William T. Kerr

In Memoriam: E. T. Meredith III (1933–2003)

All of us at Meredith Books are dedicated to providing you with
information and ideas to enhance your life. We welcome your comments
and suggestions. Write to us at: Meredith Books, New Business
Development Department, 1716 Locust St., Des Moines, IA 50309-3023.

If you would like to purchase any Meredith Books home, family, or lifestyle
titles, check wherever quality books are sold.
Or visit us at: meredithbooks.com

KEN VOSE, the writer for MONSTER NATION, is a former
race driver. He is the author of *The Car: Past & Present*,
The Convertible, and *Blue Guitar*. He has also written two
novels set in the world of Formula One racing (*Oversteer*
and *Dead Pedal*) and is the coauthor of the book and
screenplay *Greased Lightning*. He served as the writer for
INSIDE MONSTER GARAGE, also published by Meredith Books.

MONSTER GARAGE BOOK DEVELOPMENT TEAM
Thom Beers, Executive Producer, Original Productions
Clark Bunting II, General Manager, Discovery Channel
Sharon M. Bennett, Senior Vice President, Strategic
  Partnerships & Licensing
Deirdre Scott, Vice President, Licensing
Carol LeBlanc, Vice President, Marketing & Retail Development
Sean Gallagher, Director of Programming Development,
  Discovery Channel
David McKillop, Executive Producer, Discovery Channel
Jeannine Gaubert, Designer
Erica Jacobs Green, Publishing Manager

MONSTER NATION

THE BEST TRANSFORMED VEHICLES FROM COAST TO COAST

WRITTEN BY KEN VOSE

MEREDITH₀ BOOKS

Des Moines, Iowa

WHAT'S INSIDE

ME AND MY MONSTER

8

Outrageous vehicles from the backyards and garages of Monster Nation

MONSTER MODIFIERS

78

Hot rods, tuners, drifters, and more— great customized cars and the people who created them

INTRODUCTION
by Thom Beers

The popularity of Monster Garage isn't a surprise to me. I have known for quite a while that the series was part of something bigger. A whole universe of gearheads was out there, just waiting to be tapped. "Monster Nation" is as good a name as any for that bigger phenomenon. How do you know if you are a member of Monster Nation? You are if you have ever visualized changing, adapting, or customizing anything—and if you've then gone ahead and done it, executed it, you are a member in good standing. Monster Nation isn't a nation of thinkers; you've got to talk the talk and walk the walk.

Monster Nation, the title of this book, also is the name of a series that we have been producing for Discovery Channel. The shows are spinoffs of the main Monster Garage series. As this book does, the series highlights some of the most extraordinary vehicles I've ever seen and profiles the incredibly talented people who created and built them.

What makes a Monster a Monster? It's got to be cool. It has to be outrageously unique. It has to tap into the great vortex of the chrome and metal gods. What makes a Monster tick? That's the elusive essence we try to capture, whether on Monster Garage or Monster Nation. I like to say that a Monster is made by excellent craftsmen and craftswomen, and it is brought to life by means of a heart transplant: People are transplanting their own passions, their own hearts into each of these machines. That's what makes it tick, and what makes it tick differently.

The whole concept is that people are looking to define their own identity, their own individuality. They're looking to make *their* mark. It's interesting if you look back to the cowboys: every horse saddle was tooled differently. The cowboys were craftsmen at work; they had the ability to do that. But when we went to the mass-market world—when Henry Ford started cranking cars off the line—it was for cheap, affordable transportation, and that individuality went away. But the need for affordable transportation isn't the only issue now. Today a car is not just a form of transportation. A car is a form of identity. People are putting their heart and soul into their cars.

And it's not just in cars. Ten years ago, there was a big upswing in people personalizing their houses. Huge companies grew to help people do home improvement themselves. Now it's the same thing with cars: People can easily modify their own car by just picking up great aftermarket parts that are becoming more and more available. It's more accessible, and the parts are easy to install. Think about video—with cheaper cameras, everybody's a filmmaker in one way or another. It's the same thing with shop tools. Things like welders and torches have gotten accessible and inexpensive. Technology is cheaper, so people can actually afford to stock up a whole garage.

Of course, people who are personalizing their cars these days do have traditions on which they can draw, pioneers in whose steps they can follow. That's especially true here in Southern California, where we film Monster Garage and where Jesse James grew up. The old-school hot rod shops, where engine wizards added horsepower and speed, and chopped and channeled and lowered for aesthetics—that old hot rod mentality, the knowledge of what really makes a car run, has been around for a long time. And lowriders have been around for a while, too. Then you have the paint wizards like Tom Prewitt, who look at every

car as if it were a massive canvas. Beyond that, well, anybody that's got a garage, there's always one or two tinkerers in every community. They do stuff, they invent things, they're guys that love to work with their hands.

You will meet some amazing people and see a lot of incredible vehicles in the pages of this book. Check out the hot rod school bus; that's one kickin' vehicle. Talk about a slick concept! Jerry Bowers did a fabulous job on it. Then there's Rick Dobbertin's Surface Orbiter. That one will stand the test of time— it's pure, fantastic engineering. It's like a spaceship: gleaming, polished aluminum and chrome, just a behemoth. It not only looks fabulous, but it's totally functional. Dobbertin took the concept of transportation to a whole new level. He built that to drive. A lot of people build these cars to show, or to show off; Dobbertin built that car to go. He drove it down the road, he drove it in the Panama Canal, he drove it in the ocean. That is magnificent. That's a journey. That guy is like an Argonaut.

I like the part of the book about hot rods, tuners, and such. We just filmed an episode with the last remaining guys from the hot rod era of the '40s and '50s, with legends like Dick Dean, Gene Winfield,

The whole concept is that people are looking for their own individuality.

Bill Hines, and Norm Grabowski. The youngest guy on that team was 64, the oldest was 82. They chopped and lowered a '54 Chevy, and it is a beautiful car. Jesse was in heaven when we did that build.

Then there are the art cars. That's a statement—Monster making taken to the extreme. These are brilliant artists or fabricators who just see the world a little differently. Take David Crow, the guy who turned a motorcycle into a high-heeled shoe. That's just fun.

We probably hit the right time with Monster Garage and Monster Nation. Obviously, a lot of these cars already existed. But I think we're going to start seeing more and more of them. What Monster Garage has done is challenge people's imaginations. Who is Monster Nation? It's not about the young or the old; it's about anyone who takes something from his or her imagination and makes it real.

—Thom Beers
EXECUTIVE PRODUCER,
MONSTER GARAGE AND MONSTER NATION

For more about Monster Garage, visit www.Discovery.com

7

ME AND MY MONSTER

OUTRAGEOUS VEHICLES FROM THE
BACKYARDS AND GARAGES OF MONSTER NATION

ME AND MY MONSTER

RICK DOBBERTIN'S

SURFACE ORBITER

The milk truck your local dairy doesn't drive

*We were stopped seventy-eight times,
but we never received a ticket.*
— **RICK DOBBERTIN**

It has been called a DeLorean on steroids, Captain Nemo's Corvette, and a Milk Truck with Wanderlust. Rick Dobbertin calls it the Dobbertin Surface Orbiter, and he should know. He designed it, and, with the aid of more than 80 sponsors, invested nearly $200,000 in parts and 14,000 hours of construction time over a 4½-year period. Oh, and he built the 32-foot-long, 8-foot-wide vehicle inside a 39-by-13-foot garage. It was, as he puts it, "like building a ship in a bottle—and I was in the bottle with it."

While there seems to be no end of quotable, and often quite funny, stories about the Orbiter, it is anything but a joke. Between December 1993 and June 1996, the Orbiter covered about thirty thousand miles on land and three thousand miles on the open ocean, including a passage through the Panama Canal—the latter a first for an amphibious vehicle.

Who is this Dobbertin guy, anyway? Judging by the ingenious design and the quality of workmanship that went into the Orbiter, you would think he has one or more engineering degrees and wads of money. In truth, Rick is a do it yourself hot rodder with the same sort of money problems as the average DIY car guy—although, admittedly, your average hot rodder is unlikely to drive through the Panama Canal.

Dobbertin's story begins in his childhood home. "My dad," he says, "worked for General

Rick Dobbertin, hot rodder and globe-trotter.

Motors for 34 years in the finance end of it, and as a result I was always around cars. I started building Soap Box Derby cars, and that kind of stuff, when I was about eleven years old; then two-by-four and plywood go-carts with rope steering, and then carts with engines. I never went to school to learn any of it, I just did it. I learned it; I think anybody can learn it if they really want to."

Dobbertin's learning curve kept pace with his aspirations. By the time he was thirty, he had his own speed shop specializing in blowers, turbos, and nitrous oxide installations. To help promote the shop, he stuffed a twin-turbocharged 6-71 supercharged, nitrous-injected 454 big-block Chevy into a 1965 Nova SS and ended up with *Hot Rod* magazine's "1982 Street Machine of the Year." *Car Craft* called it the "car that defined the direction of Pro-Street for a whole new generation of car crafters." His next creation, a 1985 Pontiac J-2000 powered by a twin-turbo, twin-supercharged, nitrous-injected 350 Chevy, was selected as 1986 Hot Rod of the Year by *Hot Rod*. On their 50th Anniversary the

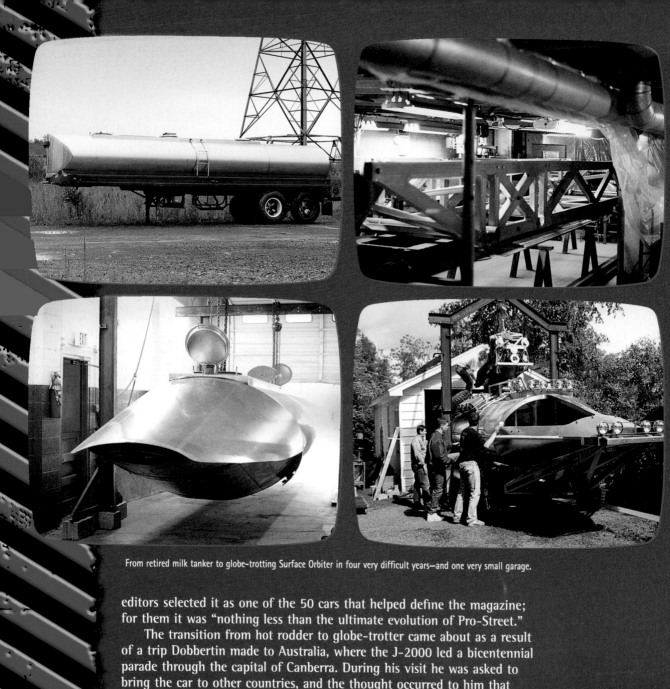

From retired milk tanker to globe-trotting Surface Orbiter in four very difficult years—and one very small garage.

editors selected it as one of the 50 cars that helped define the magazine; for them it was "nothing less than the ultimate evolution of Pro-Street."

The transition from hot rodder to globe-trotter came about as a result of a trip Dobbertin made to Australia, where the J-2000 led a bicentennial parade through the capital of Canberra. During his visit he was asked to bring the car to other countries, and the thought occurred to him that "it would be cool to just drive the car around the world. Then I thought, 'You know, I can do that.'"

A vehicle that could circle the globe would need the ability to traverse many types of terrain while on land and also be able to withstand lengthy voyages on the open seas at a reasonable speed. To Dobbertin's way of thinking, there was one obvious choice of what to use as the basis for his future Orbiter: a milk tanker.

"I selected a milk tanker," he recalls, "for many reasons. For one thing, used tankers are fairly cheap and readily available. It's made of stainless steel, so it won't corrode in the saltwater. It's small enough to be road-legal size and yet it's still big enough to deal with the ocean. It has double walls, so it's insulated, and if it can hold 30,000 pounds of milk inside, I figured it could hold the water out. So I bought one for about five thousand dollars, cut it up, and just started building." The rest, as they say, is history, but what a history.

If a quick look at the Orbiter specs is not enough to convince you that this was anything but easy, then give Jesse James a call at Monster Garage—he needs you. Consider these features:

The *vehicle body* is a 1959 Heil stainless steel tanker, double walled with 2½-inch plastic foam insulation. Its frame is constructed from 910 pieces of 304 stainless steel. It weighs in at 18,000 pounds, and it is 32½ feet long, 7½ feet wide, and 10½ feet tall. The fuel tank has a capacity of 340 gallons, and there is storage for 4½ gallons of oil, 17 gallons of coolant, and 40 gallons of water.

The *drivetrain* features a 250-horsepower, 6½-liter intercooled turbo V-8 GM engine with a Peninsular Marine conversion. There is a 4-speed automatic transmission with overdrive coupled to a 4-wheel-drive transfer case.

The *suspension* is 4-link with a panhard rod, plus air-assisted coil springs with dual shocks. Brakes include four external discs, two internal driveshaft-mounted discs, and two electric auxiliary drum brakes. The wheels are 16.5-by-9.75 aluminum, and the tires are 12.5-by-35 mud terrain radials.

By way of *electronics*, the Orbiter has dual 200-amp alternators with dual 12-volt 8D batteries and a 110-volt inverter. There's a GPS system with plotter, radar, and compasses,

> " *Think about it. It takes two people, one to drive and the other to climb out onto the roof and reach down to pay the toll.* "

and, for communication, a single-band radio, a VHF radio, a CB radio, and cellular phones.

Among its *controls,* the Orbiter has dual steering wheels—the left one for driving on land, and the right for navigating the sea—and dual shifters, with one heading into the transmission and the other to the transfer case. Thirty-two gauges, 60 switches, and 10 indicators make up the control panel.

The Orbiter's *propulsion* specs look like this: On land, it runs on part-time 4-wheel-drive with lock-out hubs and a 4.56 gear ratio, reaching a top speed of 70 miles per hour on fuel consumption of 8–10 miles per gallon. At sea, it is driven by a single 22-inch-diameter, 4-blade propeller with a 12-inch pitch and a 2.00 gear ratio, reaching a top speed of 8 knots and gobbling up fuel at the rate of 1 mile per gallon.

For *safety equipment,* Dobbertin outfitted the Orbiter with four Halon fire extinguishers, fume detectors, a life raft, and an emergency position indicating radiobeacon (EPIRB), along with a strobe, flares, and five-point seat belts.

Toss in air conditioning, heaters, keel coolers for the engine, transmission, and oil, a bow thruster, fore and aft winches, a floor window, 8 boat fenders, 6 spare tires,

The GM powerplant awaits installation.

and 4 spare Lexan windshields—by now you have one well-outfitted Monster amphibian.

The interior of the Orbiter is laid out with a front compartment housing the controls, communication and navigation equipment, and storage; a middle compartment has an engine room, sleeping quarters, and additional storage; and a rear kitchen compartment has a sink, microwave, water heater, restroom, and more storage. It is registered for land use as a "Custom House on Wheels" and on the water as the motor yacht *Perseverance*.

Once the Orbiter was up and running—and floating—Rick and his then wife set off on what would be a three-year odyssey that would take them through 38 states, 28 countries, and the Panama Canal, before a shortage of meaningful sponsorship brought the project to a halt. Dobbertin had to cover most of the expenses associated with the trip on a pay-as-you-go basis.

"I had these photo cards of the Orbiter made up," he recalls, "and I'd sell them for two or three bucks apiece, literally. That's how I financed the trip. I'd have zero money, zero fuel, pull off at a rest stop, get out with a pile of them, sell fifty dollars worth in about twenty minutes, go get gas, and then sell a

few more to get something to eat. We never made any money; it was just trying to make ends meet.

"Another way I got some money was to drive into a town on a Wednesday or Thursday, find a car dealership, and offer to park the car on their lot for the weekend for an agreed upon fee, with the understanding that if I didn't get at least one newspaper and one TV story out of it, then it was free. It never missed."

Although Dobbertin's plan to drive and sail completely around the world did not work out, he did make it to such far-flung places as the Bahamas and Central and South America. There were any number of unusual adventures along the way.

"There was one woman in the Bahamas," he remembers, "who refused to leave her home for weeks because she was convinced we were from another planet. From there we went to the Dominican Republic and nearly caused an international incident: People thought we were a U.S. attack submarine on maneuvers in their territorial waters and staged a huge protest in front of the American Embassy. In Puerto Rico the DEA searched the Orbiter for drugs. They were upset because we had sailed all the way

RICK DOBBERTIN'S HYDROCAR

The success of the Orbiter convinced Rick Dobbertin of the viability of amphibious transportation and led directly to his new project: The HydroCar. The HydroCar, currently being fabricated in Dobbertin's shop near Syracuse, New York, takes the lessons learned on the Orbiter and translates them into what will be a revolutionary vehicle.

Scheduled for completion in 2004, the HydroCar is a stainless-steel-tube-framed chassis covered with marine-grade aluminum. It's made in three sections with the cockpit, engine, and drivetrain in the middle and moveable, foam-filled sponsons on either side. Eight air bags raise and lower the sponsons. The upper position is for use when driving on the road while the lower turns the HydroCar into a catamaran with three underbody hydrofoil wings to provide additional lift. The wheels are raised and lowered via a second air-bag system that allows them to be concealed inside the sponson wheel wells for reduced drag.

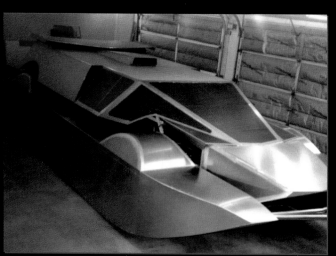

Changing from land to water mode is done with a dash-mounted switch. Powered by a 572-cubic-inch, 620-horsepower Chevy V-8, the HydroCar is expected to reach 125 miles per hour on land and 50 miles per hour on the water. Dobbertin pegs the cost at an estimated $150,000. ◎

A group of heavily armed back-road "toll collectors" in Colombia stopped Dobbertin—and asked to have their picture taken with the Surface Orbiter.

from the Dominican Republic without being detected by their surveillance planes and ships. The police in St. Thomas thought we were a Colombian semi-submersible drug smuggling boat. Then, when driving through Colombia, we got stopped by heavily armed guards who wanted us to take their pictures with the Orbiter. It was quite a trip."

Of all of the mishaps, only one had near-fatal consequences. On the voyage from the Dominican Republic to Puerto Rico in 18-foot seas, the Orbiter suffered a series of mechanical failures that led to a mayday call to the Coast Guard, who in turn alerted a nearby freighter, which began a search for them. The Orbiter sits so low in the water that, as the DEA had discovered, it is nearly invisible. As a result, the five-hundred-foot freighter nearly rammed them, coming so close that it tore off the left rearview mirror.

But, according to Dobbertin, the most difficult part of traveling in the Orbiter has nothing to do with storms at sea, armed guards, or drug agents. It's stopping at a tollbooth. "Think about it," he says. "It takes two people, one to drive and the other to climb out onto the roof and reach down to pay the toll. Then there's the increased interest by the state police and the toll-road authorities, sometimes accompanied with the attitude of, 'You're not going to drive that thing through my state, are you?' We were stopped seventy-eight times, but we never received a ticket." ⚙

The Surface Orbiter on its way through the Panama Canal.

Swamp Buggy

EPISODE 3 - **VW BEETLE SWAMP BUGGY:** Rick Dobbertin had four and a half years, 80 sponsors, and nearly $200,000 plus 14,000 man-hours to build an amphibious vehicle that would be equally at home on interstate highways and the open ocean. Jesse James and the crew at Monster Garage might have thought that was cool, but they were looking at a tougher amphibian challenge—fabricate a swamp buggy that would take on a genuine swamp boat head-to-head in the Louisiana swamps, and do it in just five days with only three grand. The Monster's machine? A stock VW Beetle handled by none other than Jesse himself. The opponent? A 400-horsepower, big block Chevy

engine mounted on a custom-built aluminum boat body piloted by a professional named Ronnie Thibodaux, who's been cruising the wetlands of Louisiana for some 28 years.

Jesse wanted the Beetle to work like a boat but still look like a Beetle when they were finished. "This one," he said, "was pretty tough—tough to make it float and still keep it semi-stock looking." Swamp boats are equally at home on land and in the water. The land part was easy. The water part was another story. The engine had to slide in and out of a trunk only 66 inches deep. The team decided on a 110-horsepower, air-cooled VW engine driving 14-inch carbon-fiber aircraft-propeller blades and rudders. They fit the engine in by

removing the rear seat, the trunk panels, and most of the rear fenders and body. Making the car float was another issue. The fenders were filled with AB flotation foam and the entire undercarriage was plated with sheet aluminum and then tightly sealed. Jesse added a prow, and when they drove the Beetle into the water it floated like a rubber ducky in a bathtub.

How'd they do in competition? It was a close race, but Jesse crossed the finish line first because all he had to do was drive the bug into the water and start motoring, while Robbie lost precious time unloading and launching his machine. Another Monster win! ◉

Upper left: Jesse welds the frame for the prow onto the front of the Swamp Buggy. Upper right: Jesse at work. Lower left: It started stock but that's not how it ended up. Lower right: The finished Swamp Buggy gets a flashy coat of red paint.

ME AND MY MONSTER
HYLER BRACEY'S
BIG HORN

KAHLENBERG

All the bells and
whistles—and then some

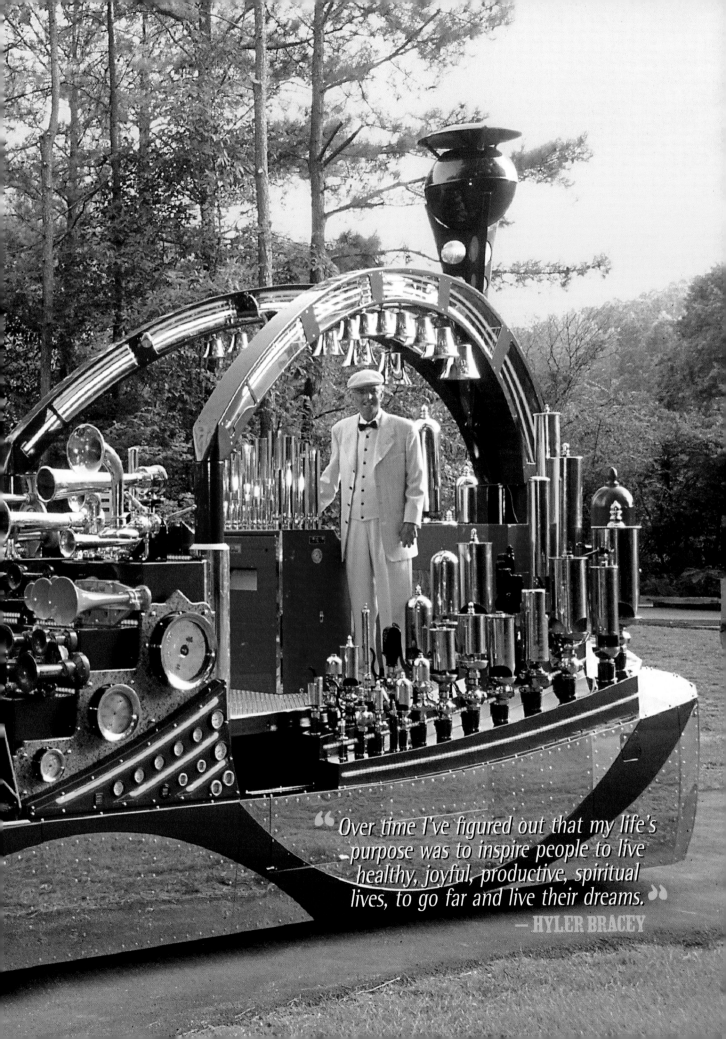

" *Over time I've figured out that my life's purpose was to inspire people to live healthy, joyful, productive, spiritual lives, to go far and live their dreams.* "

— HYLER BRACEY

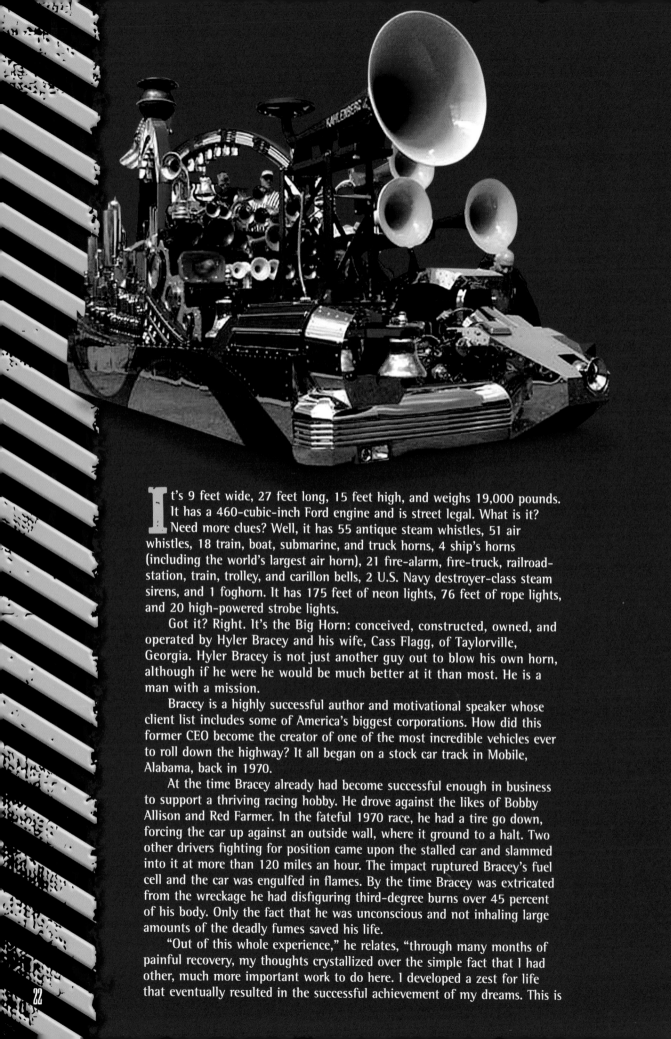

It's 9 feet wide, 27 feet long, 15 feet high, and weighs 19,000 pounds. It has a 460-cubic-inch Ford engine and is street legal. What is it? Need more clues? Well, it has 55 antique steam whistles, 51 air whistles, 18 train, boat, submarine, and truck horns, 4 ship's horns (including the world's largest air horn), 21 fire-alarm, fire-truck, railroad-station, train, trolley, and carillon bells, 2 U.S. Navy destroyer-class steam sirens, and 1 foghorn. It has 175 feet of neon lights, 76 feet of rope lights, and 20 high-powered strobe lights.

Got it? Right. It's the Big Horn: conceived, constructed, owned, and operated by Hyler Bracey and his wife, Cass Flagg, of Taylorville, Georgia. Hyler Bracey is not just another guy out to blow his own horn, although if he were he would be much better at it than most. He is a man with a mission.

Bracey is a highly successful author and motivational speaker whose client list includes some of America's biggest corporations. How did this former CEO become the creator of one of the most incredible vehicles ever to roll down the highway? It all began on a stock car track in Mobile, Alabama, back in 1970.

At the time Bracey already had become successful enough in business to support a thriving racing hobby. He drove against the likes of Bobby Allison and Red Farmer. In the fateful 1970 race, he had a tire go down, forcing the car up against an outside wall, where it ground to a halt. Two other drivers fighting for position came upon the stalled car and slammed into it at more than 120 miles an hour. The impact ruptured Bracey's fuel cell and the car was engulfed in flames. By the time Bracey was extricated from the wreckage he had disfiguring third-degree burns over 45 percent of his body. Only the fact that he was unconscious and not inhaling large amounts of the deadly fumes saved his life.

"Out of this whole experience," he relates, "through many months of painful recovery, my thoughts crystallized over the simple fact that I had other, much more important work to do here. I developed a zest for life that eventually resulted in the successful achievement of my dreams. This is

where Big Horn fits into the picture. My hope is that somewhere in my story others can find the hope and inspiration to achieve their dreams and visions."

For Bracey, the sound of large horns was a part of his growing-up experience. As a high school student in Port Arthur, Texas, he had a part-time job as a deckhand on a tugboat.

"The massive sounds of boat horns were a constant part of my workday, and I grew to love each one of their distinctive notes," he says. "So it was only natural that eventually these sounds would work their way back into my life."

The beginnings of the Bracey horn collection began innocently enough with a remark made by his wife. "We had bought a motor home," Bracey says, "and Cass got in an encounter where a car got in her way, and then when she blew the horn it was just this little 'beep-beep,' and she said, 'I'd like a horn that says *get out of my way.*' So, remembering those tugboats, I'm thinking to

myself, 'Wouldn't it be neat to have a boat horn?' I went to the library and couldn't find any books about horns. I did find a manufacturer and ordered a boat horn, which we put on the roof. Then I got some more horns, and a train whistle, and put them all on the roof. Now we could make all kinds of noise going down the road. It was when I was doing all of this research that I came across a man in Detroit who had another train whistle for sale, and when I talked to him he said that if I was so excited about buying a train whistle I should buy his horn truck. And I did—sight unseen."

"It had three ship's horns," he continues, along with "ten or fifteen train horns, boat horns, and maybe five or six whistles, and it was one ugly truck. We fixed it up, trying to make it more attractive—Cass says it was like putting lipstick on a pig. But we started taking it out, doing festivals and things, and having fun with it."

As more and more requests came in for the truck to make appearances, it became

Hyler Bracey with the original Big Horn.

obvious that driving this now-12,000-pound vehicle was not going to work. The solution was to put it into an enclosed trailer and haul it behind a bus that had been converted into a motor home.

Shortly after he read about the launching of a new navy ship, the USNS *Big Horn,* Bracey contacted the captain. When the ship docked at the Norfolk Naval Base there was a meeting of the two Big Horns. But the pleasure of that illustrious event would turn to despair within a matter of days; early one morning on the trip home disaster struck.

"I looked in the mirror to check traffic," Bracey relates, "and was shocked to see the trailer pulling out to the left side of the coach. Suddenly it disappeared from view. I looked in the other mirror and saw it skidding out of control across the interstate, air brakes on all six wheels firmly locked. The trailer broke free, cleared the traffic lane to the far right, flipped on its side, and slammed into the embankment."

While, thankfully, no one was injured, the truck was almost completely destroyed. Fortunately, most of the horns survived,

Upper left: Bracey visits the U.S. Navy's own *Big Horn.*
Upper right: The overturned trailer in which the original Big Horn came to grief. Lower left: Inside the trailer. Lower right: Hyler and friends with the design for the current Big Horn.

but for Bracey it seemed like the end of his dream.

"I was depressed," he says. "I had never been so depressed in my life. I was talking it over with Cass, and she said, 'So what do you teach people about what happens when their dreams get tossed?' I said, 'Well, there's always some opportunity.' And I realized God had given us a blank piece of canvas—that we could now really create something truly magical." That something is the current Big Horn, the one with, as Bracey puts it, "all the bells and whistles."

In addition to all of those bells and whistles and horns and sirens, Big Horn also has an Allen-Bradley Programmable Logic computer to control all functions; more than 200 Allen-Bradley switches and controls; more than 10,000 feet of wire to more than 3,000 connections; 66 electronic and mechanical gauges, including 6 antique steam gauges;

a 7,500-kilowatt Onan 110-volt generator; 7 gel cell 1,000-amp batteries; a 2,500-watt Heart inverter; 16 electric motors; and 2 smoke machines.

The design of the current incarnation of Big Horn is the result of a competition among students in the School of Industrial Design at the University of Cincinnati. Twenty-one students submitted their proposals to Bracey, Cass, and six other judges. The completed Big Horn is testimony to the brilliance of the winning design by Kristen McKinley-Steiner.

But when it was time to turn Kristen's design into reality—time to start the build, as they say on Monster Garage—the process was no piece of cake. As Cass relates: "Looking at the design picture, we said, 'Let's put the engine here in the front where it probably needs to be.' And we had a milk crate, I mean this was very scientific—we're saying, 'Yeah, that looks right.' And as we

> **"***The only part that is not custom-made is the engine and transmission. The rest of it was cut, piece by piece, and put together.***"**

went along people kept contributing. We modified and added a lot more than the original. The only part that is not custom-made is the engine and transmission. The rest of it was cut, piece by piece, and put together. We thought it would take about a year and cost maybe $100,000. And after the first year we didn't have a whole lot to look at—mostly a frame—and we kept writing checks." The amount of work needed to complete such a massive and complex vehicle was enormous. What was planned to take just one year took about five years.

Having learned their lesson with the accident to the original Big Horn, it was decided to make a custom tractor-trailer rig that would house the new one, along with living space for Bracey and Cass. The rig, made by Champion Trailer in Texas, is almost as impressive as its unusual payload.

One final piece of the puzzle was yet to be completed. In order to drive this mighty

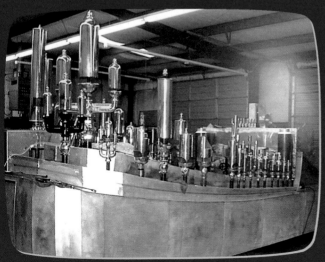
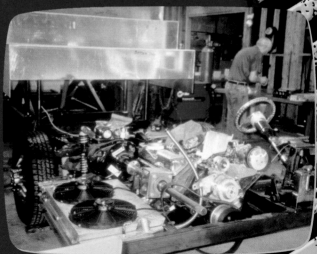

transporter, Bracey and Cass each would need a commercial driver's license (CDL). Bracey says that he is as proud of completing the eight-week CDL course and passing his test as he is of his Ph.D. Oh, and he was so nervous during the exam that he nearly omitted a key part of the test: He almost forgot to blow the horn.

"I thought what would happen was that I would use it in my speaking career. And the reality is that you can't get this 19,000-pound, 27-foot-long thing in a hotel room, although I've made speeches where it's been on display at a minor league baseball stadium. And yet I use it in every speech that I do and it serves me well. So maybe I just needed to build it—to create this thing to inspire other people." ☼

27

Revs Up to the Altar

EPISODE 16 – CHEVY SUBURBAN WEDDING CHAPEL:
Hyler Bracey's Big Horn is a testament to his zest for life and the embodiment of his goal to inspire others to fulfill their dreams. And it's loud, which is what Jesse James wanted when Monster Garage accepted the mission of converting a Chevy Suburban into a wedding chapel complete with a birdseed thrower and an in-vehicle pipe organ/calliope. ("I want it loud," he said, and he meant it.) The first order of business was to hinge the rear passenger doors from the bottom to create a walk-through vestibule and hinge the roof to create an arch above the vestibule so the happy couple could stand with the minister for the nuptials, scheduled to be performed in the marriage capital of the world, Las Vegas, Nevada, on Valentine's Day. Of course a happy couple and a minister willing to do this had yet to be discovered, but that was a minor detail. The real challenge was designing, fabricating, and fitting into the Chevy a working calliope powered by nitrous oxide tanks, especially since it had to lie flat for driving and swing up into position so it could be played during the ceremony by a veteran of thirty years on the Queen Mary, Jaqlyn Flory. Jesse fabricated the calliope swing mechanism while the rest of the team fitted the doors and worked the interior. It wasn't an easy

build; tempers flared during construction and again while waiting for the calliope to be finished. But when Jaqlyn sat down to play, it was loud and Jesse smiled. A contest was held to pick the lucky couple, and Jesse spent some time on the Internet ordaining himself as a minister. Everybody met in Vegas, and Jesse asked the bridegroom if he would take the bride as his "old lady." He said yes, Flory rocked on the Monster calliope, and the party didn't break up until 4 a.m. ◉

Upper left: Building the organ took longer than expected, which frayed some tempers as the deadline approached. Upper right: Jaqlyn Flory wailing some wedding tunes on the calliope. Lower left: The vestibule arch was much easier to fabricate than the gull-wing rear doors, which were initially so heavy the actuators wouldn't raise them into position. Lower right: All's well that ends well—Jesse beams in the background as the couple seals it with a kiss.

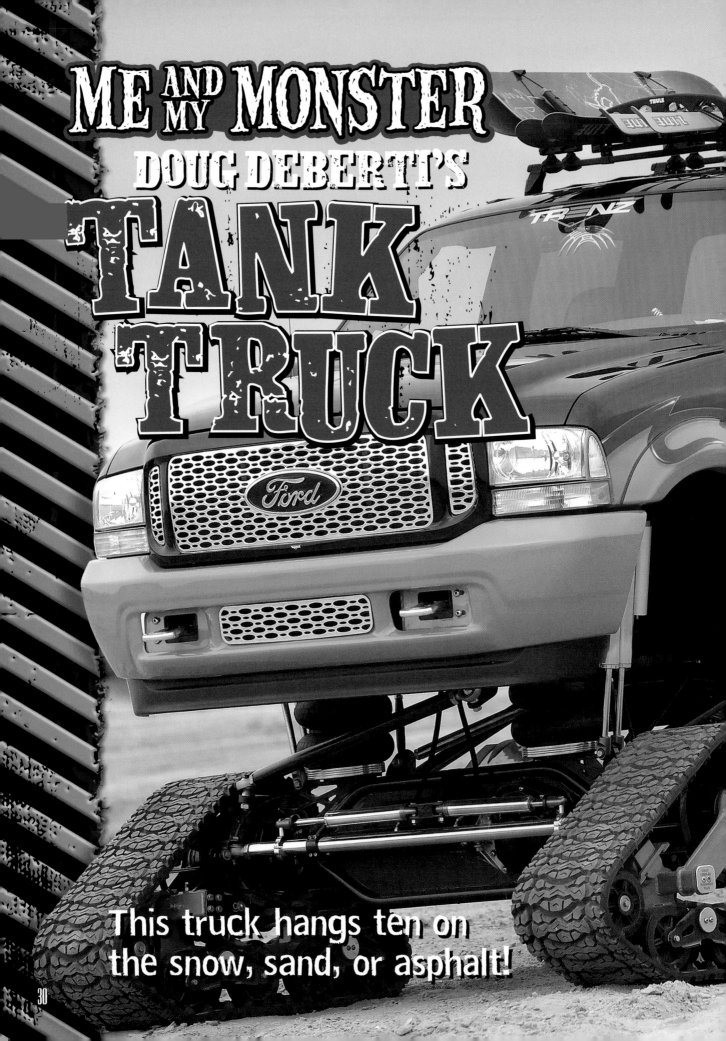

ME AND MY MONSTER

DOUG DEBERTI'S

TANK TRUCK

This truck hangs ten on the snow, sand, or asphalt!

"What I really like doing is the one-off stuff. I'm most creative in coming up with something really different. We have our own style. I refuse to copy anything. I like our stuff to stand out."

— DOUG DEBERTI

In November 2003 the city of Las Vegas hosted the 37th annual Specialty Equipment Manufacturers Show, or SEMA as it's known in the automotive world. SEMA is unlike any other auto show in the country and about as close to gearhead heaven as you're likely to get. It's for the trade only, with more than 5,000 booths featuring everything from the biggest, baddest Hummers to guys hawking weirdly scented air fresheners. Once pretty much a gathering of aftermarket suppliers, it also has become an arena where the big three vie for the attention of the 75,000 attendees with customized versions of their latest vehicles. These prototype "show" cars are now produced almost entirely by outside contractors—high-end custom shops numbering in the hundreds that create their own versions of the standard Ford, GM, or Mopar offerings.

The custom shops compete with one another for various design awards presented by the manufacturers during the show. The winners invariably show up on magazine covers, in feature stories, and on television. One of the most successful of this new

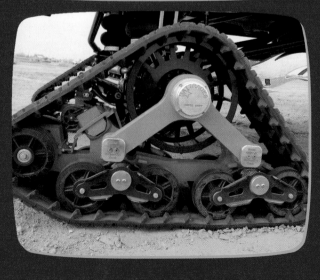

Whether it's the custom-tooled billet aluminum steering wheel, the immaculate leather upholstery, or the unique Mattracks half-tracks, one-off is what DeBerti's style is all about.

breed of customizers is Doug DeBerti, the founder and owner of Trenz in Bakersfield, California. He was awarded Ford's Best of Show in 2001 for the SkyScraper, his version of the Ford Excursion; in 2002 it was Ford's Best Design award for the radical F-350 Tank Truck; and in 2003 he won both Best of Show with a modified T-Bird and Best Design for his Ford Iron Man F-150 "Tonka" pickup. Not bad for a guy who headed for California 18 years ago with two hundred dollars in his pocket.

When DeBerti graduated from high school, he did what countless others before him had done: He packed his stuff into an old truck and motored west. The trip from Butte, Montana, to Bakersfield, California, was measured in more than miles; it was the start of a new life for the 18 year old. At first that new life consisted of flipping burgers, pumping gas, and working as a roughneck on an oil-drilling rig.

Working on trucks in his spare time—first his own, then others'—DeBerti began to make a name for himself building parts, making lowering kits, and getting the job done and done right. He named his new venture California Truck, but he still had to work another job to make ends meet.

"I'd get up real early, work my other job on the oil rig, and be at California Truck from about ten in the morning until eight at night," he says. "I did that for about four years until, finally, California Truck started to take off. I needed money to put into the business, so I applied for a bunch of credit cards, got four of them, and quit the other job. That's really what I started with: four credit cards."

He expanded, opening a second California Truck outlet as well as a smaller shop in which he began to manufacture customized billet aluminum grilles. The robust sales of these high-end items convinced him that this was the way to go.

> *"I needed money to put into the business. That's really what I started with: four credit cards."*

DOUG DEBERTI'S FORD TONKA TRUCK

DeBerti takes his toys seriously. "We tried to keep the truck as close to stock-looking as possible but give it a plastic look. Even the interior looks like a Tonka toy. When you open the hood you can't see the motor, just the plastic. This one is not like some of the others that are great to look at but you wouldn't want to drive them every day. Everybody who sees this wants to get in and go."

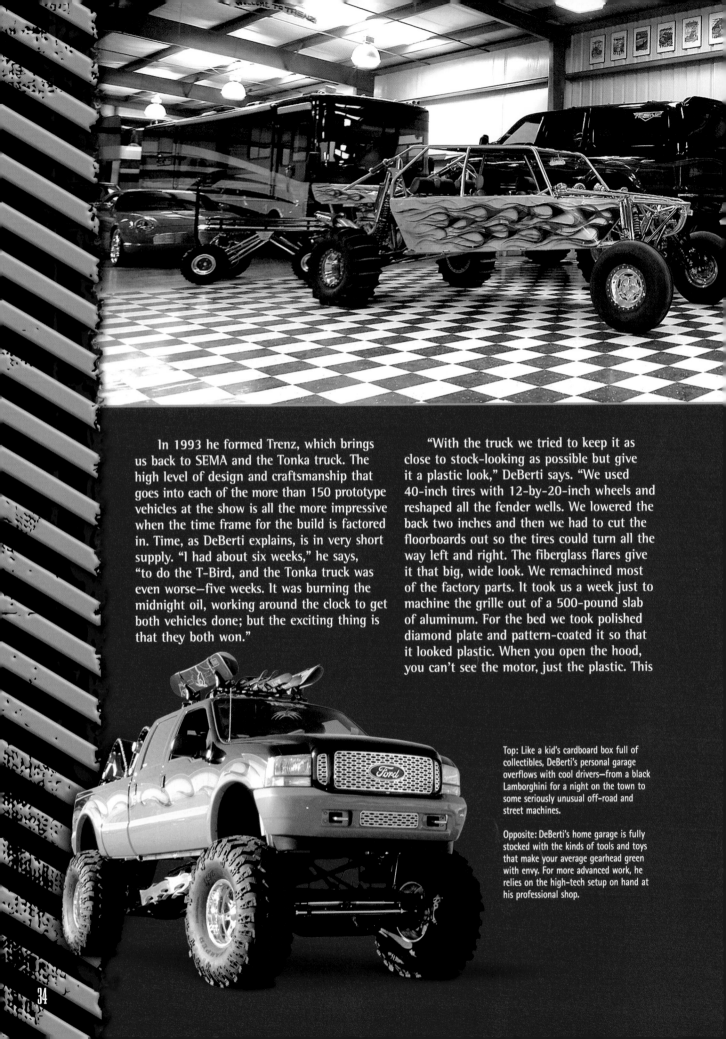

In 1993 he formed Trenz, which brings us back to SEMA and the Tonka truck. The high level of design and craftsmanship that goes into each of the more than 150 prototype vehicles at the show is all the more impressive when the time frame for the build is factored in. Time, as DeBerti explains, is in very short supply. "I had about six weeks," he says, "to do the T-Bird, and the Tonka truck was even worse—five weeks. It was burning the midnight oil, working around the clock to get both vehicles done; but the exciting thing is that they both won."

"With the truck we tried to keep it as close to stock-looking as possible but give it a plastic look," DeBerti says. "We used 40-inch tires with 12-by-20-inch wheels and reshaped all the fender wells. We lowered the back two inches and then we had to cut the floorboards out so the tires could turn all the way left and right. The fiberglass flares give it that big, wide look. We remachined most of the factory parts. It took us a week just to machine the grille out of a 500-pound slab of aluminum. For the bed we took polished diamond plate and pattern-coated it so that it looked plastic. When you open the hood, you can't see the motor, just the plastic. This

Top: Like a kid's cardboard box full of collectibles, DeBerti's personal garage overflows with cool drivers—from a black Lamborghini for a night on the town to some seriously unusual off-road and street machines.

Opposite: DeBerti's home garage is fully stocked with the kinds of tools and toys that make your average gearhead green with envy. For more advanced work, he relies on the high-tech setup on hand at his professional shop.

one is not like some of the others that are great to look at, but you wouldn't want to drive them every day. Everybody who sees this wants to get in and go."

DeBerti's Tank Truck is definitely not a daily driver, unless perhaps you live in the Alps. *Truckin'* magazine called it a "totally wazoo, over-the-top, jaw-dropping, in-your-face custom," and they know a thing or three about custom trucks. DeBerti wanted to do something wild to top his winning Excursion, so he had automotive artist Craig Fraser (see page 150) come in to help put his outrageous concept on paper. The design immediately got the go-ahead from Ford, and the fun began.

DeBerti started by removing the entire stock suspension system, replacing it with a set of huge air bags and a four-link suspension setup. Using a water-jet laser cutter he created solid 2-inch-thick dagger four-link bars. All four of the daggers were polished over a 34-hour period at a cost of $6,000 per trailing arm, and then attached to QA1 Teflon-coated Heim joints. The system also includes King Racing shocks and Air Ride Technologies air valves, pumps, and digital gauges. With this setup the ride height can be controlled with the truck in motion, whether on wheels or on its unique Mattracks half-tracks. The truck is street legal with the

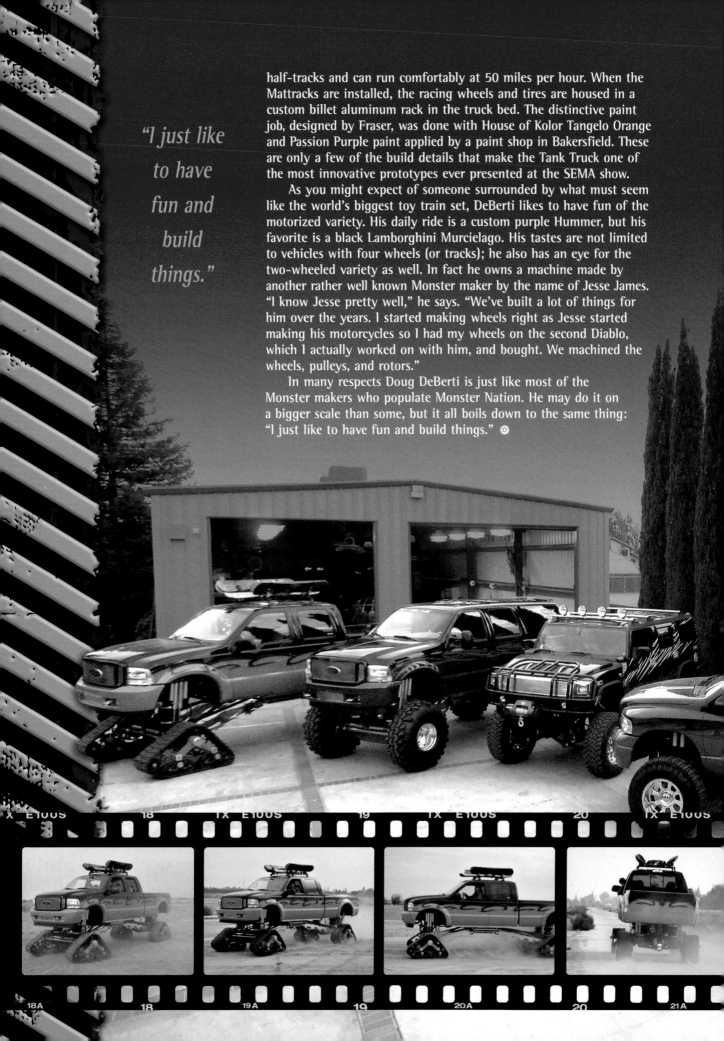

half-tracks and can run comfortably at 50 miles per hour. When the Mattracks are installed, the racing wheels and tires are housed in a custom billet aluminum rack in the truck bed. The distinctive paint job, designed by Fraser, was done with House of Kolor Tangelo Orange and Passion Purple paint applied by a paint shop in Bakersfield. These are only a few of the build details that make the Tank Truck one of the most innovative prototypes ever presented at the SEMA show.

As you might expect of someone surrounded by what must seem like the world's biggest toy train set, DeBerti likes to have fun of the motorized variety. His daily ride is a custom purple Hummer, but his favorite is a black Lamborghini Murcielago. His tastes are not limited to vehicles with four wheels (or tracks); he also has an eye for the two-wheeled variety as well. In fact he owns a machine made by another rather well known Monster maker by the name of Jesse James. "I know Jesse pretty well," he says. "We've built a lot of things for him over the years. I started making wheels right as Jesse started making his motorcycles so I had my wheels on the second Diablo, which I actually worked on with him, and bought. We machined the wheels, pulleys, and rotors."

In many respects Doug DeBerti is just like most of the Monster makers who populate Monster Nation. He may do it on a bigger scale than some, but it all boils down to the same thing: "I just like to have fun and build things." ☼

"I just like to have fun and build things."

DOUG DEBERTI AND TRENZ

During the past ten years DeBerti and Trenz have gone from being a small maker of aftermarket custom billet grilles for trucks to a state-of-the-art computerized manufacturing facility. Trenz makes billet wheels, license frames, dash kits, billet machined mirrors, doorsill plates, billet steering wheels, office furniture, extreme toys for kids, and radical designs for trade-show booths—as well as custom hot rods, motorcycles, cars, and trucks. Even DeBerti seems surprised at the way things have gone.

"We have a 35,000-square-foot building and employ a little over a hundred people," DeBerti says. "I've designed over 3,000 parts that we mass distribute everywhere. We're now machining parts around the clock seven days a week. Last year I merged Trenz in order to grow the business and also started DeBerti Design and DeBerti Products. What I really like doing is the one-off stuff. I'm most creative in coming up with something really different. We have our own style. I refuse to copy anything. I like our stuff to stand out. I'm lucky. I have an awesome wife and two boys, nine and twelve—both of them as creative as can be. My twelve-year-old, Shane, already designed a rearview mirror that is in production right now—it's pretty cool."

Top: DeBerti's daily driver, a radical purple Hummer.
Bottom: This robot welder is typical of the
state-of-the-art equipment employed at Trenz.

MONSTER GARAGE™

Deflated Dream

EPISODE 29 - DELOREAN HOVERCRAFT:

In the prototype fabrication business, time is always against the builders. Deadlines hover and the pressure increases with each passing day. Time is a taskmaster Doug DeBerti knows something about—he built both his prize-winning T-Bird and the Tonka Toy Truck in a matter of weeks. Jesse James knows a little about pressure. He faces it every week on Monster Garage, and it drives him to be a winner. But he's a practical man and knows teamwork is crucial—one week to complete a Monster build means that the team has to work together like a well-oiled machine. And though the team is chosen because they're experts, Jesse's the man and they have to stick with his program and listen to what he says. In the case of Episode 29, the DeLorean Hovercraft build... well, they didn't listen very well.

Jesse had some doubts about the project from the start. He didn't know much about hovercrafts, and he never was the biggest fan of the DeLorean. The challenge was to turn the car into a hovercraft while keeping its stock appearance. Jesse laid out the plan and left the garage—his mistake. When he got back he found that the team had taken the easy way out, stripping the body parts off the DeLorean frame and simply attaching them to the hovercraft body. Jesse was unhappy, and one of the team members departed. A day and a half had been lost, but Jesse insisted they start from scratch—one man short. With Jesse in charge, the team worked hard to meet the challenge, but the DeLorean Hovercraft never got off the ground—or the water. What do you do to ease that sense of failure? For starters, you let a U.S. Army team grind the machine into chunks with an amphibious assault vehicle. And just to make sure it happened right this time, Jesse went along for the ride. ⚙

Upper left: A genuine U.S. military hovercraft delivers the amphibious assault vehicle that will give the DeLorean what it deserves. Upper right: Jesse dons some combat gear in preparation for the assault. Lower left: The assault vehicle takes care of business. Lower right: The results.

ME AND MY MONSTER
DEAN JEFFRIES'S
LANDMASTER

Shock and awe—
Hollywood style

We built it to run through walls, tear up buildings, go through just about anything. The steel in the nose is 3/8 inch thick.
— DEAN JEFFRIES

Dean Jeffries was a stand-in for Frankie Avalon in the 1960s film *Bikini Beach Party*. Had he done nothing else in his life, you wouldn't be reading about him here. Fortunately for him (and you), that is not the case.

In 2001 Jeffries was inducted into the Cruisin' Hall of Fame, in recognition of a body of work that spans more than three decades. During that time he built some of the wildest vehicles on the planet. They include: the Monkeemobile, the Green Hornet's Black Beauty, the moon buggy from the James Bond flick *Diamonds Are Forever,* all the wild vehicles in *Death Race 2000,* and the incredible Landmaster.

The Landmaster was built for the movie *Damnation Alley,* which starred George Peppard and Jan-Michael Vincent. The 1977 film was about a band of people who survive a nuclear holocaust and travel across the desert seeking safety. Although *Damnation Alley* is rarely seen today, its star vehicle, the Landmaster, lives on prominently in a lot of people's memories.

After its cinematic debut, however, the Landmaster rusted away for decades in the storage area of Dean Jeffries's Hollywood Hills studio/garage, waiting patiently for the

Dean Jeffries poses in front of the Mantaray, currently on display at the Petersen Museum in Los Angeles. "It now seems like a crime to have torn apart a rare Maserati, but back in '63 it wasn't worth a thing," says Jeffries. Mantaray won the Tournament of Fame at the Oakland Roadster Show in 1963. The radically customized sports car garnered acclaim in custom automotive circles but, after a chance appearance on the old Steve Allen show, it also launched Jeffries's long and successful Hollywood career as a stunt coordinator and fabricator of fantasy movie rides.

audition that might never come. But, in true Hollywood fashion, there is indeed a happy ending to the story. Recently the Landmaster has been restored to its former glory, and the mighty vehicle is once again wowing fans of innovative fabrication and design as they're done in the Dean Jeffries style.

Weighing in at 11 tons, and probably more when it's soaking wet, the 35-foot-long monster was constructed over a three-month period out of steel and aluminum. And while a lot of movie magic is just that, the Landmaster is the real thing. "We built it to run through walls, tear up buildings, go through just about anything. The steel in the nose is ³/₈ inch thick," says Jeffries proudly. "The Landmaster can do a lot of things," he continues, "and if you hit a hole it just walks right over it." During filming of *Damnation Alley* the Landmaster, traveling at more than

50 miles an hour, slammed down a 25-foot drop and kept right on truckin'.

This Monster is at home in the water, too. It's waterproof enough to navigate the waters of a good-size lake. Other "standard" equipment includes six remotely operated cannons, two armor-piercing bazookas, closed-circuit television, a radar scanner, two bunk beds, and a bathroom with shower.

Powered by a 391-cubic-inch Ford truck engine, modified with Crager headers and an Edelbrock manifold, the Landmaster can clip along at highway speeds. (At one time the machine was licensed for highway use in California.) It has enough torque to handle the roughest terrain.

"Not much will stop it, but this thing works better at 40 miles per hour than 15. When you get up to 30 or 40, everything smooths out."

The Landmaster rides on 38-inch farm-equipment tires mounted on 12 special 16.1-inch wheels. Just in case you weren't paying attention, that's 12 wheels. Mounted in triangular sets, the gear-driven wheel assembly operates with two wheels on the ground and the third above. The unique design is based on a tri-star wheel arrangement that Lockheed designed some years back for military all-terrain vehicles. The tires are driven by a system of "star gears" around the axle. All three tires rotate continuously during operation but only two of each set are on the ground at any one time.

If the vehicle is stymied by an obstruction, the third wheel in each set rotates down to add traction and pull the vehicle out. "The Landmaster has no springs, no suspension," says Jeffries. "If you hit something it just flips up and goes over it. If you get stuck in the mud, you can lock the wheels and the tri-star will dig itself right out. You can go in water,

Everywhere you look under the shell of the Landmaster you see steel, steel, and more steel. This movie-star-in-the-making needed the extra beef in order to handle the real-world requirements of *Damnation Alley*. The triangular tire assembly makes the big Ford engine look small. Jeffries boosted the size of the radiator and cooling system to ensure that the Landmaster wouldn't break down during shooting for *Damnation Alley*. It didn't.

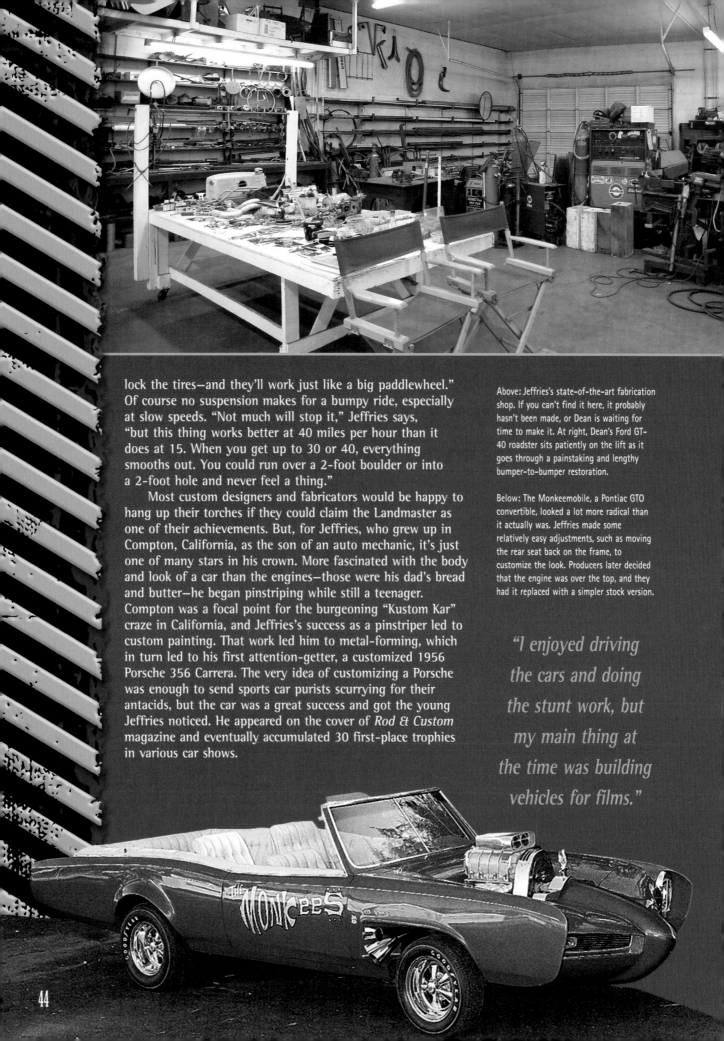

lock the tires—and they'll work just like a big paddlewheel." Of course no suspension makes for a bumpy ride, especially at slow speeds. "Not much will stop it," Jeffries says, "but this thing works better at 40 miles per hour than it does at 15. When you get up to 30 or 40, everything smooths out. You could run over a 2-foot boulder or into a 2-foot hole and never feel a thing."

Most custom designers and fabricators would be happy to hang up their torches if they could claim the Landmaster as one of their achievements. But, for Jeffries, who grew up in Compton, California, as the son of an auto mechanic, it's just one of many stars in his crown. More fascinated with the body and look of a car than the engines—those were his dad's bread and butter—he began pinstriping while still a teenager. Compton was a focal point for the burgeoning "Kustom Kar" craze in California, and Jeffries's success as a pinstriper led to custom painting. That work led him to metal-forming, which in turn led to his first attention-getter, a customized 1956 Porsche 356 Carrera. The very idea of customizing a Porsche was enough to send sports car purists scurrying for their antacids, but the car was a great success and got the young Jeffries noticed. He appeared on the cover of *Rod & Custom* magazine and eventually accumulated 30 first-place trophies in various car shows.

Above: Jeffries's state-of-the-art fabrication shop. If you can't find it here, it probably hasn't been made, or Dean is waiting for time to make it. At right, Dean's Ford GT-40 roadster sits patiently on the lift as it goes through a painstaking and lengthy bumper-to-bumper restoration.

Below: The Monkeemobile, a Pontiac GTO convertible, looked a lot more radical than it actually was. Jeffries made some relatively easy adjustments, such as moving the rear seat back on the frame, to customize the look. Producers later decided that the engine was over the top, and they had it replaced with a simpler stock version.

"I enjoyed driving the cars and doing the stunt work, but my main thing at the time was building vehicles for films."

His next attention getter was the Mantaray, which was built on a modified Maserati chassis. When he and the car appeared on the Steve Allen television show, they were noticed by the folks in Hollywood and soon made their screen debuts with Jeffries doubling for Frankie Avalon while driving the Mantaray. "I doubled for Frankie Avalon with a wig and makeup and all that junk. But it got me going in the movie business," says Jeffries. "Before I knew it I was building vehicles for the movies. The first one was the moon buggy used in the James Bond film *Diamonds Are Forever.*"

This quickly led to even more movie work. Before long Jeffries was working as a stunt driver and coordinator on films like *What's Up Doc?, Damnation Alley, Fletch, Romancing the Stone,* and *Honky Tonk Freeway,* where a miscalculation by Jeffries resulted in the price a stuntman pays for such mistakes—a broken back.

By the mid 1970s Jeffries was considered to be one of the top constructors and drivers working in the motion picture business. Says Jeffries, "I enjoyed driving the cars and doing the stunt work, but my main thing at the time was building vehicles for films."

Maybe the Monkeemobile didn't need the extra drag but the parachute did add a certain amount of class. A monster wind must have been blowing down N. Cahuenga the day this photo was shot.

What is arguably the most famous of his vehicles was actually done for a television series, the bright red Monkeemobile. Jeffries took two stock Pontiac GTO convertibles and within three weeks he had produced two Monkeemobiles: one for television production and one for taking around to car shows.

The Monkeemobile looks radical, but the changes were less drastic than their overall appearance might suggest. Jeffries left the wheelbase alone, but he made the car appear to be stretched by moving back the rear seat. He stood the windshield up to nearly vertical and put on an old-fashioned touring top. The big-block, supercharged engine jutting up through the hood packed enough horses to pop wheelies. After a while, however, the producers decided the engine look was too aggressive and reinstalled the original engine.

Another Jeffries television car was the Black Beauty that was piloted by the Green Hornet and his faithful sidekick Kato (the young Bruce Lee). Black Beauty was based on a 1966 Chrysler Imperial with a 440 engine and automatic transmission.

These days Jeffries spends a lot of his time working on one of the most remarkable cars of the past fifty years, the Ford GT-40. Of the few GT-40s that were built during the years that Ford contested the Le Mans 24 Hour Race, only four were roadsters, and Jeffries has one of the two survivors left today. Jeffries has had the vintage racer for more than 30 years, and he's still tinkering away on it to this day.

"When I got it," he says, "it had a small-block automatic and was set up as an engineering test mule with three sets of motor mounts." It's a different story these days. Valued at somewhere north of fifteen million dollars and rising, the project has much of the gearhead world waiting eagerly to see the restored car. Jeffries isn't in a hurry to pull it off the lift. In true rodder fashion, he has no plans to put the GT in a museum—he'd rather drive it. As he puts it, "Cars were made to be used, and, besides, it didn't cost me fifteen million." ◉

Behind the wheel of the Landmaster and ready to rock and roll, Jeffries raises the doors in preparation for a spin around the desert.

"Cars were made to be used."
—Dean Jeffries

Below: Getting the Landmaster trailered up for the trip to *Damnation Alley* was the first test of the tri-star wheel assembly. It obviously worked.

Above: The Black Beauty carried some heavy fantasy weaponry. The car was created for the *Green Hornet* television series and started out as a 1966 Chrysler Imperial. Below: The Mantaray was a Maserati before the ultimate customizer, Dean Jeffries, turned it into something from another planet.

MONSTER GARAGE™

Delivers Access

EPISODE 28 - ACCESSIBLE MERCEDES:

This build proved that Monster Nation has room for everyone—and that Monster Garage could take a serious subject seriously and still turn out a stylin' ride for a physically challenged driver.

Jesse wanted a vehicle that fit the requirements for wheelchair accessibility and fully hand-controlled driving without sacrificing great design and a full assortment of Monster goodies. To get the job done, he gathered a team of experts willing to leave their egos at the door and make things happen. In fact, two of the team members motored around on wheelchairs themselves, so they knew the territory firsthand.

Jesse wanted the driver to fit behind the wheel without having to get out of the chair;

the team decided that the best entry would be a rear-of-car motorized ramp and fold-down lift— a door design much like the left-front driver's door on the Dean Jeffries Landmaster (see page 46). This entailed a gut job on the Mercedes that would make most fabricators give up. But the Monster team jumped in with torches sparking. They cut up and rebuilt much of the main frame to allow a chair to pass from front to back with plenty of headroom. They removed the driver's seat and lowered the frame and deck so the driver could slide under the wheel and lock the chair securely in place. After the hand controls were installed, they cranked the motor. They found clearance adjustments on the deck necessary to get the universal joint turning without obstruction—and soon the Benz was purring like a kitten. ◉

Upper left: Jesse uses the English wheel to shape a cover for the differential, which was exposed after the deck was lowered. Upper right: Getting a chair inside meant lowering the Benz's frame several inches. Lower left: Installing the access ramp. Lower right: Twenty-five-year-old Shawn Tobin got the surprise of his life when Jesse showed up and told him to take a spin.

Below: Jesse demonstrates how the lift is lowered from the rear of the ride. When Shawn first saw the car, he couldn't believe it was an accessible vehicle. Later he got a bigger shock when Jesse told him the monsterized Benz was his to keep, no strings attached.

ME AND MY MONSTER

BEAU BOECKMANN'S

KOFFIN KRUZER

AND THE ULTIMATE TAILGATER

One is cool enough to make
the grim reaper smile...
and the other is hot enough
to make a hot dog squeal

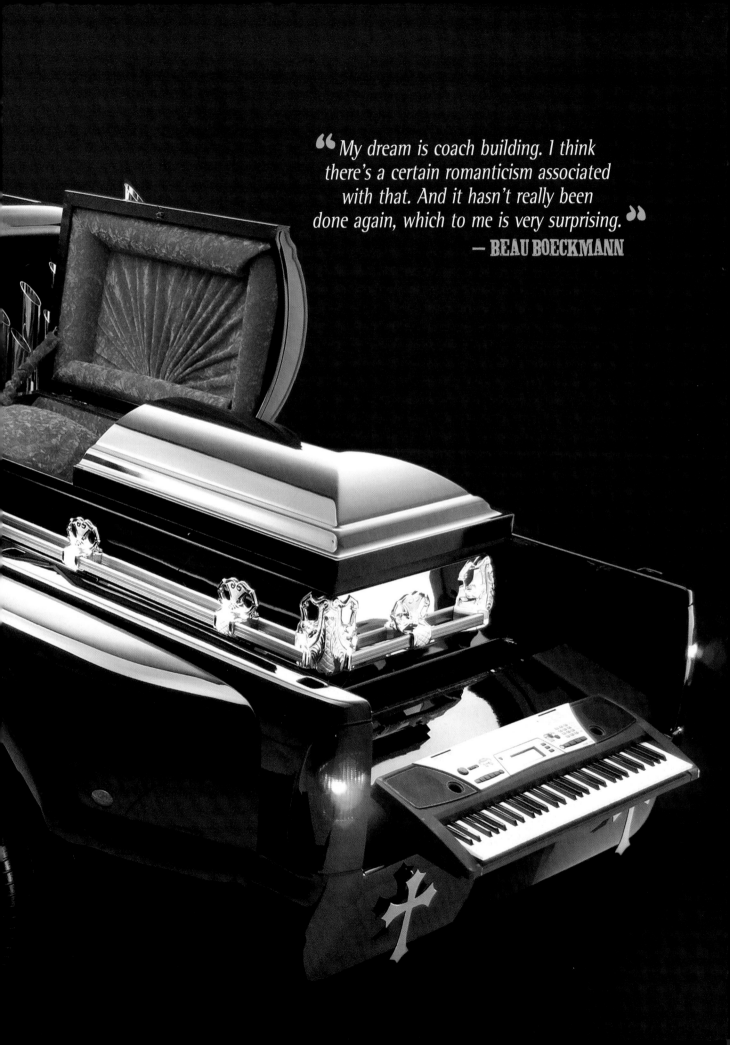

"My dream is coach building. I think there's a certain romanticism associated with that. And it hasn't really been done again, which to me is very surprising."
— BEAU BOECKMANN

Beau Boeckmann has built a lot of custom cars and trucks. His personal favorite is the Koffin Kruzer. The Kruzer, says Beau, is "an F-250 with a totally custom-built truck bed that holds a real coffin and a working pipe organ. We actually built the pipes right behind the cab, and the speakers play through the pipes so you get that real deep, deep pipe sound. We took the crushed red velvet interior of the coffin and matched that to the interior of the cab, which is also done in crushed velvet. We also have a McIntosh stereo system for that old-school look; it's really *bad*." The Kruzer is on display at Galpin Motors in Southern California, right alongside a fleet of other so-good-they're-*bad* Galpinized vehicles.

Galpinized? When Bert Boeckmann, president of Galpin Motors, began customizing vans about forty years ago, he coined the word as a replacement for "customized" (which was customarily used by customizers). His son, Beau, who is the vice president and chief designer, has turned out dozens of Galpinized vehicles, including the Koffin Kruzer.

"My father noticed back in the '60s," says Beau, "that kids were fixing up vans, so he did one with a special paint job, put in wood paneling and carpet, and the 'surfer van' as they called it back then was born. Then a friend who loved camping came along, and he designed a van for him with a refrigerator, a sink, wardrobe—even a toilet. That was the first real conversion van, and it started the whole conversion van business.

"I'm 33 now and I practically grew up at the dealership. My father's been there for fifty years. He started as a salesman, worked his way up, and eventually bought the company and grew it into the number one Ford store in the world. So I grew up there, always seeing these really cool custom cars. I got my first car when I was 15. My grandmother willed me her 1965 Mercedes 220SE. I totally restored it. Did a black-lacquer paint job with a black interior. I found some leopard-skin material that had been in storage for decades and put it in

Beau Boeckmann, vice president and chief designer at Galpin Motors, with one of his custom tailgaters.

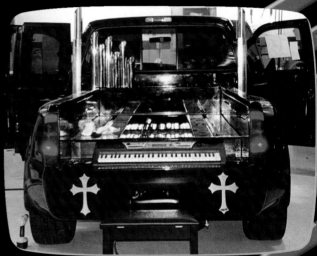

there and, as strange as it sounds, it turned out gorgeous. I never thought of customizing as different; it was always part of my life. I don't think I've ever had a stock-looking car."

Although the customized, uh, Galpinized, vehicles account for only a small portion of the dealership's overall sales, they are, as Beau points out, the ones that get noticed in publications like *The Wall Street Journal* and *Architectural Digest*.

"At any one time," according to Beau, "we'll have two or three hundred customized vehicles for sale, and then we have our wild creations which we do for our annual calendars, various promotions, and car shows. They get people's attention and show what can be done when you're only held back by your own imagination. I have a real passion for automobiles and customizing, and I want to be as creative as possible in helping people realize their dreams."

Those attention-getting vehicles have included a Gucci Thunderbird, a Pinto with a fish tank in the back, the Evel Knievel Gladiator F-150 SuperCrew Pickup, the Star-Spangled Mustang, the Mercury Lowrider, two different Tailgate Party Trucks, and the Koffin Kruzer.

Just as the '60s surfers had to have that perfect woody or conversion van, today's young hot shoes are into tuner cars. And they're not all testosterone-fueled either; Boeckmann finds that as more women want tuner cars, their influence is being

felt in the marketplace: "Hey, women have better taste than men for the most part, so why wouldn't they be listened to? My girlfriend's 10-year-old daughter, Amelia, came up with the idea for our Pink Champagne Jaguar XK8. It has pink pearlescent paint, matching pink pearl leather interior, and a pink burl wood dash."

"When it comes to tuners," he says, "we have a Focus-based 'Tearor' tuner, a supercharged SVT with a paint job that looks like it's going so fast it's tearing itself off the car. It's orange and green, so it's in really sharp contrast. We did the same thing in the interior—actually took the seats and just tore up the materials, tore it all to shreds, and then put it all back together. It has an ultimate sound system with three bass speakers, eight high-end speakers, and subwoofers in pods modeled after nitrous oxide bottles. It also has two TVs and a DVD player."

Another of Boeckmann's radical tuner cars is called The Glow. It's a Mazda Protégé 5 with actual neon winding its way around the seats, doors, dash, gearshift, wheels, and

undercarriage. The Kenwood sound system features a 450-watt amp running two 7-inch Excelon subwoofers built into a glowing neon box. If you're wondering what kind of kid could afford a creation like this, the answer is simple: the 40-year-old kind.

Beau Boeckmann's way of looking at how the automobile can be tailored to the wants of the individual owner almost seems like a throwback to designers in the 1930s like "Dutch" Darrin, or Figoni et Falaschi.

"My dream," as Boeckmann puts it, "is coach building. I think there's a certain romanticism associated with that. And it hasn't really been done again, which to me is very surprising."

"You get shops," he continues, "that specialize in one particular area like the tuners, the off-roads, or the stereo shops, but no one's really taken it to the next step and put it all into one place—and that's what we're really out to accomplish with what we call Galpin Auto Sports, or GAS. It will be a center with a very large showroom and with a design area where you can actually plan every detail

Just a few of the vehicles that Boeckmann has "Galpinized."

of your car down to different styles of paint—flames, scallops, whatever. It will all be right there in one location. We've got a very creative and energetic team here who work on all of this together. We really have fun."

Where do you go if you want to get the ultimate truck for that big Super Bowl tailgate party you're planning? Monster Garage? Well, Jesse and the crew certainly built one major tailgate party monster (see page 58), but unless you're personally invited to BBQ with Jesse you won't be flipping any burgers on that truck. You could buy a grill and put it in the back of your pickup, but that's not going to impress anyone. Or you could go to Galpin Ford and check out all the goodies on the Galpinized F-150 Party Truck: a fiberglass bed cover that lifts hydraulically to the height of the cab, bringing two 22-inch flat-screen TV monitors with it; a full-size stainless steel propane grill with all the utensils; a pouring station and a sink with running water; two ice chests, one for keeping beverages cold and the other for storing ice and food; a full-size blender; a DVD player with bed-mounted speakers; and a satellite dish. About the only thing it doesn't come with are Galpinized hot dogs.

Are you ready to get Galpinized? ☸

The ultimate tailgater: Beau Boeckmann's F-150 Party Truck.

MONSTER GARAGE™

Car-B-Que

EPISODE 31— CADILLAC ESCALADE TAILGATER: Jesse James spared no expense when he set out to build the ultimate tailgate machine. This one was so far over budget they could have financed two Monster builds, but the result made eyes pop when it was unveiled at a pro football game in San Francisco in the fall of 2003. Jesse wanted the machine to look absolutely stock with a cool paint job and great detailing when it rolled into the parking lot, so that fans would be blown away as the beast magically transformed itself into remote-controlled party central. The transformation would involve five basic elements essential to successful tailgating: a kick-butt sound system, a Monster gas-powered barbecue grill, food and beverage service, a 42-inch plasma television with satellite hookup, and a game-station control module—all of which would roll out on motorized platforms from various parts of the car via remote control. The design team decided that the food and beverage service would roll out the back, the plasma TV would hang from the tailgate door, the barbecue grill would appear from the rear passenger door, the sound system would be installed in the rear side windows, and the game-station control module would be housed behind the driver's seat. The challenge for the build team? Make it happen! The team consisted of experts in the fields of hydraulics, high-end

audio/visual, and, of course, welding. As usual, the build started with gutting the Escalade's interior to make room for the customizing to come. This group of guys was a well-oiled machine, each doing his thing and solving problems as they came up. When Day Five arrived, everybody got a toolbox and a handshake from Jesse for a job well done. Then it was off to the stadium for the ultimate tests— were the brats hot, the speakers loud, and the beverages cold? The answer in all cases was a resounding yes. ⚙

Upper left: Installing a roll-out platform. Upper right: Twenty-six-inch wheels with custom Jesse James rims make the Caddy welcome on anybody's team. Lower left: The Escalade Tailgater is open for business. Lower right: A very scary linebacker appears out of the flames on the hood.

ME AND MY MONSTER
JIMMY TROTTA'S
I SCREEEEM TRUCK

Two scoops of hell raisin' with sprinkles on top

" *My main message is love. I try to profess peace in every aspect. I always encourage my brothers and sisters to party in peace.* "
— JIMMY TROTTA

Big Twin magazine called him "Louis Armstrong dressed in flames," and said that "Seeing him in his red and white outfit, riding his Servi-car three wheeler and ringing his bell like crazy, is like watching the Tournament of Roses parade minus the horses." While both of those descriptions are true, they barely prepare you for the nonstop, explosive antics of the person they describe. He may have been named Jimmy Trotta by his parents, but he is known to the rest of the world as The Ice Cream Man from Hell.

Whenever bikers gather at places like Sturgis, South Dakota, Daytona, Florida, or Laconia, New Hampshire, the Ice Cream Man is there, exhorting people at the top of his lungs with his signature call: "Ladies and gentlemen, how about some ice cream?" How does a guy who makes Marlon Brando's Wild One look positively timid end up selling ice cream of all things? "I saw," Trotta says, "an ad in the paper that said, 'Good cash business. Interested parties please call.' I did, and went around to see this guy who had two ice cream trucks, and he told me how he'd put himself through college selling ice cream. It sounded good to me. I'm a pretty persistent fellow so I decided to give it a try. No sooner did I get the trucks back to my garage than another guy came over, saw the trucks, and said, 'Jim, do you know how much money there is in ice

> *" I knew then that my wife and I were in the ice cream business. "*

cream?' That did it. We cleaned one truck up, painted it white, made it as pretty as we could, and named it 'Anna's Ice Cream Truck' after my wife. The first time we tried it we sold out in four hours, and not one of those kids gave Anna a check. I knew then that my wife and I were in the ice cream business."

Once he was fully established in his new venture, Trotta took things to the next level: He turned a Harley into an ice cream bike.

"After a couple of years of proving that I'm serious about this, I said, 'Anna, I want to build a Harley Davidson ice cream trike out of a serving car.' So we found an old police bike, took it home, and I did my voodoo magic on it. I've been a motorcycle and hot rod builder for years. I love auto bodywork, rebuilding, chopping, everything like that. So I did it."

A short time later, at a bike rally in upstate New York called AMJAM, Trotta was out early one morning pushing popsicles when a biker took one look at him and said, "Oh, my God. It's the ice cream man from hell." For Trotta, those words would prove to be life changing. "The light bulb went off. I know how powerful a name change is; from Attila the Hun [and after], people have done it—had their name changed and realized the power in it. I just realized the same thing. I also know that the only way to the subconscious is through repeated orders through your

conscious mind. So I said the name to myself over and over and over again, and one morning I woke up and I believed it."

These days the Ice Cream Man often can be found behind the wheel of a chopped and sectioned 1954 Chevy ice cream truck with a blown 454 motor, an air-bag suspension system, and a radical flame motif.

Trotta built the truck, but the inspiration came from none other than Ed "Big Daddy" Roth. When the two met at the New England Summer Nationals in 1992, the truck was still pretty much stock. But after Roth executed some sketches for him, Trotta went to work, turning Big Daddy's vision into reality. "Ed was a real cool cat. Meeting him... I was like a kid in a candy store. I mean, that's the guy that I used to color in his coloring books, wear his key chains, everything—he was IT!"

The Ice Cream Man may be from hell but nowadays he is in great demand for things like birthday parties and graduations. Kids love the outrageousness of it all. "They all want bragging rights that The Ice Cream Man from Hell was at my house. Parents love it too. I have a family that comes down from Canada every year for bike week, and from the time that they could carry their child, who is now about fourteen, they wanted pictures of the stages of his life standing next to the Ice Cream Man. I deliver good memories."

Although The Ice Cream Man from Hell may look like one tough guy, he's never been affiliated with any outlaw motorcycle club. This is hardly surprising given his chosen line of work and his philosophy. "My main message," he says, "is love. I try to profess peace in every aspect. I always encourage my brothers and sisters to party in peace." Ladies and gentlemen, how about some ice cream? ⚙

ME AND MY MONSTER

JERRY BOWERS'S
HOT ROD SCHOOL BUS

WANNA BE COOL...STAY IN SCHOOL!

You'll never be late
for school again

"Then we started chopping.
We didn't measure or anything.
It was just kind of, 'That looks good.'"
— JERRY BOWERS

Seeing, as they say, is believing, but when what you're seeing is the Hot Rod School Bus it still takes some getting used to. The bus, which was conceived and created by hot rod builder Jerry Bowers of Magnolia, Delaware, has been traveling across the country for the past five years bringing a message to the schoolchildren of America: If you want to be cool, stay in school.

It's certainly not your run-of-the-mill school bus. "I was driving on Wilshire Boulevard in Santa Monica," said one person to Bowers, "and when I saw your fine machine, I almost plowed into some parked cars." Another said: "I teach high school in San Jose and my first thought was 'We need one of those.' That is the coolest school bus in the world, hands down."

Bowers had originally named the bus Low Life High, but when he saw the way kids were taken with it he realized that the name was sending out the wrong message. "We're doing lots of things with kids," he says, "and the word 'lowlife' had some bad connotations. So we changed it to Shortcut High, and everybody loves it." Here's another testimonial: "We saw your bus in Ocean City, Maryland, and my daughter, who is now five, said when she starts school she wants your bus to be the one she rides in."

Shortcut High, which began life as a standard Ford school bus, is the culmination of a lifetime of dreaming, tinkering, and constructing one-of-a-kind machines. Bowers,

who grew up on a small farm in Edinburgh, Virginia, was customizing cars well before he was old enough to drive. "We were poor farm people," he relates. "We had plenty to eat and everything but toys and stuff like that, we basically made our own. That's what started me working with my hands, messing with Revell models. I had a '56 Ford and I did everything to it that could possibly be done— then did it over and over again. I took pieces of wood to extend the fenders, crayons for dummy spotlights, wire for lake pipes, and stuff like that.

"One of my dreams was to make a living designing cars, but you really need to go to college and we couldn't afford that. While I was in high school I took industrial arts, and the instructor saw that I had some artistic ability and suggested that I pursue that. I knew that people wouldn't pay me to draw cars, but they would pay me to letter their signs. When I got out of school I got a job in a sign shop, and that's what I've been doing the rest of my life. Of course I built a few cars along the way."

The list of cars Bowers built runs the gamut from a '37 Chevy coupe at age 16, to various Plymouths, a T-bucket roadster, and a couple of Mercs, including one he was particularly fond of: "It was a '53 four-door sedan. It was our family car. I slammed it down, took spray bombs and panel scalloped it—made it real radical looking. When it turned it would really kick butt. Then there

Chopped and "slammed down," Shortcut High packs a lot of punch in its height-challenged frame.

The journey from junkyard to schoolyard took Jerry Bowers five years. Most of the original sheet metal had too many coats of paint on it, so Bowers replaced it with new aluminum. Bowers reduced the length of the original bus by removing three of the vehicle's 27-inch sections.

was a '70 Chevy short-bed pickup with a Z-28 motor. Of course I slammed it on the ground. That sucker would run. It would pass everything but a gas station."

The idea for the bus came up at a car show in Maryland. Bowers was talking with some other rodders when he wondered aloud why no one had yet chopped or lowered a school bus. "So I thought," he says, "this could be pretty darn cool; OK, I'll go and do it. I knew it had to be chopped, it had to be lowered—slammed down. And my goal was that the bus itself would be five feet high."

Bowers bought an old, retired bus and towed it to his shop to begin its five-year makeover. "So we had this thing," he says, "and it was atrocious. I mean, it was a project. First thing we did was to start tearing it up. It was built in 27-inch segments so we took three segments out of the center, pushed the rear end forward, and folded it back together. Then we started chopping. We didn't measure or anything. It was just kind of, 'That looks

good.' Now it was still on the original frame, and my plan was to fabricate a rectangular tube frame for it, when this friend who had a salvage yard told me that a Cadillac Eldorado frame would work. It was great: front-wheel drive, which eliminated the driveshaft hump in the floor and saved a ton of work. "One night we got about a dozen people down there and we jacked up the body, pulled the frame out from underneath, slid in the Caddy frame, and dropped it back down." As for the doors, "I wanted to retain the original floppy doors, and to get them down to size I had to make about nine different kinds of cuts."

Over the course of the five-year build Bowers was lucky enough to have a support group of family and friends who gave up weekend after weekend to make Shortcut High a reality. "A friend up in Michigan finished off the doors. Both of my brothers—so many, many, people who came out and worked their butts off. My girlfriend, Brenda—without her this bus would not be." ◉

Too Kool for Skool

EPISODE 8 - SCHOOL BUS PONTOON
BOAT: Jerry Bowers
built Shortcut High to travel around and tell
kids it's cool to stay in school. The Monster
Garage team has nothing against education (in
fact, they're for it), but when they decided to
turn a yellow school bus into a pontoon boat
they were thinking more about what the old
alma mater would look like from the rearview
mirror than through the windshield. Their goal
was simple: build the ultimate floating party
wagon complete with a barbecue grill; take a
relaxing cruise on Lake Havasu; and have a
race with some civilian pontooners. First they
cut the roof down the middle, welded on some
tubing and sheeting for strength and to keep
the water outside, added some piano hinges so
the sides would swing down, and laid flotation
foam in the sides of the bus that would
become the pontoons. Then they rigged a
pulley system to raise and lower the pontoons
and added another pontoon to the front to
keep the engine dry. To make the thing move
in the water, they welded a motorcycle
sprocket on a driveshaft connected to a
propeller with a motorcycle chain, so that the
propeller could be powered by the bus
accelerator. Easy? Not! Jesse said the build
"was hard because of the sheer amount of
labor. Doing such a big thing took a six-guy
crew. It was a big project." But it ended in
success. The bus performed perfectly, so
perfectly, in fact, that when the civilian
competition smelled the grill heating up they
forgot about the race and joined the Monster
team on the Monster bus. ◉

Upper left: Jesse makes sparks cutting some metal reinforcing for the pontoons. Upper right: Welding the structure to hold the pontoons together. Lower left: The team tests the piano hinges that will anchor the pontoons as they're raised and lowered by the pulley system. Lower right: The pressure's on, but there's always time to lighten things up.

KOOL BUS

ME AND MY MONSTER

SCOTT OWENS'S

DB DRAG RACER

Ohio Generator
HIGH-AMP ALTERNATORS

The truck that'll blow your ears as well as your mind!

"Our number one goal is to set a world record in our class and to win first place. Our number two goal would be to win the Extreme Cup as the loudest car in the world."

— SCOTT OWENS

One of the young people vying to become top dog in dB drag racing— the master blaster of the universe—is Scott Owens, owner of Edge Audio, a custom shop dedicated to building advanced audio demonstration vehicles. Owens has been involved in the mobile electronics industry for more than 11 years, and he has been participating in competitive sound events since 1998. Owens, who is 30 years old, lives in Tempe, Arizona, with his wife, Trish, and two children, Cort and Harly.

"When I was in college I needed a summer job," says Owens. "I ended up at a stereo shop and I just never quit. I started doing demo cars, mainly for local stores so that they could have something to show off—so when people came in they'd have something besides a wall of speakers to stare at. They could actually sit in the car and see what the capabilities were. I got involved to the point where I was building cars for various sound competitions, and that led to my working with Precision

It takes a lot of power to hit a 173.3 dB high note, and the Owens truck has it in spades.

dB DRAG RACING

The spectators sitting in the wooden bleachers fell silent as the two cars awaited the signal to start. Both cars were empty and buttoned up tightly, every nook and cranny sealed to prevent sound from escaping. The teams, nervous with anticipation, had done everything they could to prepare. As the announcer completed his countdown, the familiar "Christmas tree" lights flashed, the giant digital clock activated, and, with two almost simultaneous "burps" of sound, it was all over. Team Superior's Ford Pinto had won the semifinal heat with a dB level of 173.7. As the crowd applauded, the jubilant crew pushed the winner back into the recesses of the huge Nashville Convention Center to prepare for the finals—the chance to prove once again that they were indeed the loudest car on the planet. The what?

If you haven't yet heard of dB drag racing, you will. It's way too loud to be ignored. Started in 1995 with a single meet, it has grown to encompass more than 800 events with 36,000 competitors in 54 countries. What is dB drag racing, and why in the world would anyone want to have a car stereo system capable of producing more than 50,000 watts of power and making more noise than a 747 does at 50 feet?

Basically, in dB (for decibel) racing two competitors go head to head to see who has the loudest car stereo system. The vehicles are placed side by side. A sophisticated high SPL (sound pressure level) sensor is placed inside each vehicle. Each competitor then has thirty seconds to activate his or her system and score the loudest SPL. This is not about music. This is about NOISE—noise that can be heard only as a sort of rumbling, buzzing hum to those outside the vehicle. Inside it's another story, one that no one with an ounce of sense would want to experience.

For the audio manufacturers, who now support the sport in much the same way that other corporations sponsor stock-car racing, it's a chance to prove to a growing number of fans that they are indeed the best, or at least the loudest. It's also a place to test their new products before putting them into what has become a seven-billion-dollar-a-year marketplace—the theory being that if it will stand up to this abuse, it will last you the rest of your natural life.

For the competitors, it is a chance to excel in a "sport" where few have gone before. Wayne Harris, the man who founded dB drag racing, knows where they're coming from—he came from there himself. "The vast majority of these competitors," Harris says, "are everyday kids that live down the street from you. They're high school or college age, into cars and music and girls. Some of them work in car stereo shops, but mostly they're just kids who love music and love their cars. They're the same way I was a long time ago—they don't just want to listen to stereos but they want to draw attention to themselves."

While it's true that the majority of people involved in the sport are low-buck competitors using their everyday drivers, it is still competition. And as they say in every other form of racing, "How fast do you want to go? How much do you want to spend?" No one knows this better than Harris. "The competitors here, at the World Finals, are the elite. Almost everyone is getting some kind of support, except for the street vehicles where sponsors are not allowed."

Scott Owens's workspace.

Power, Inc., in Phoenix, where I helped build the Alma Gates Bronco."

With Owens as team manager, the Gates Ford Bronco won a number of titles and broke a world record in 2000. The Bronco is still on the competition audio circuit, but primarily as a show and demonstration vehicle. It is one of the few vehicles that spectators can sit in when the power is applied. It may not operate at full volume anymore, but it will still make your hair stand on end.

In January 2001, Scott started his own business, Edge Audio. In May 2002, he began building a vehicle with which to pursue a new dB drag racing SPL (see box, page 73) world record. Sponsored by Pioneer Electronics, the completed Ford F-250 truck is something to see—and hear. It features 3 Ohio Generator alternators, 9 Pioneer 12-inch TSW5000 series woofers, 36 Rockford Fosgate BD1500 amplifiers, and 72 Turbostart 16-volt batteries, all of which work together to put out an amazing 54,000 watts of power.

"When they first came to me about building this vehicle," he says, "I told them I wasn't interested. It's too much work, it costs too much money, and it takes too much time. And they're never done. It's exactly like a race car. It's never done. There's always something that has to be changed on it—something that has to be built, has to be better—because if your whole goal is product recognition you've got to win, to be on top.

"Anyway, I ended up doing it and it's working out well. It's fun. We're in the very top pro class. I'm not sure, but I think there are only maybe twenty or thirty in this class in the whole world. It's extremely expensive. My amps are over $1,000 each, the subwoofers are close to

"It's exactly like a race car. It's never done. There's always something that has to be changed on it."

Top: Inside the air-ram-operated door are cylindrical baffles in which the woofers will be mounted.
Bottom: The steel superstructure that replaces the truck's front dash.

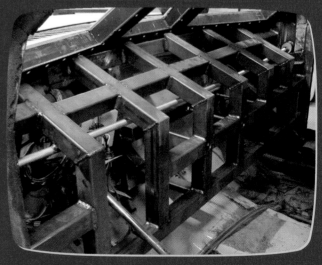

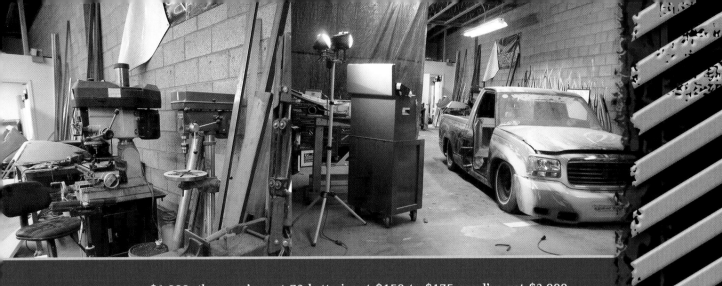

$1,000, then you've got 72 batteries at $150 to $175 per. I've got $3,000 worth of copper connecting the batteries. It's outrageous.

"Just to make the truck play with no spare equipment or anything, just amps and speakers, I've got over $50,000 in it. And I have to have spare equipment. I had to build the truck. There's over $40,000 in materials in that truck. The windshield alone, which is made of 2-inch plexi, cost $5,000.

"Our number one goal is to set a world record in our class and win first place. Our number two goal would be to win the Extreme Cup as the loudest vehicle in the world. It costs a lot of money to do that—to really do it right. Some other competitors say, 'You're getting paid—you suck.' I don't understand what they're talking about. I don't do this stuff for free. I'm sorry, but this is not a hobby. I get paid to do it, and that's the way it is."

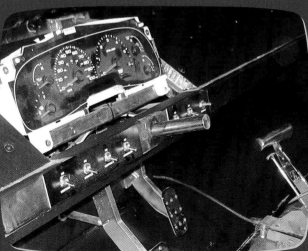

> *"The truck is full of concrete— there's probably 4,000 pounds in there."*

Fans of Monster Garage would have felt right at home if they had witnessed the conversion of the stock Ford F-250 into a 17,600-pound, 54,000-watt Monster. What would have surprised them, however, is that Scott pretty much built it by himself. "Every once in a while," according to Owens, "I'll have people come by and help when there's stuff that's just too big to move, but ninety-five percent of the time it's just me."

As with a typical Monster Garage build, the first question to be answered was, as Owens puts it, "What type of vehicle? Now in the class we're in, the top class, we were going to need lots of equipment, and what would best hold all that equipment? I think a four-door, super-duty, long-bed truck is going to hold a lot of stuff. So we got the F-250."

And then, in true Monster Garage fashion, the build began with some ripping, cutting, tearing, and shredding: "The first step was to tear it apart. I started," Owens says, "by kicking out windows and cutting steel out of it—I mean, I cut. People can't believe how much you can cut out of a car. I don't think I've ever built a show car that I didn't cut metal out of. I do put a lot of structural stuff back in so that it ends up stronger than it was originally. My welding skills are up there. It's going to be strong. I started building it in May 2002, and by the time it was done it had taken about five months."

Upper left: The Owens team before their world finals victory. Lower left: The winning SPL reading. Upper right: Getting ready for the Deathmatch competition. Lower right: Owens, right, being congratulated for his Deathmatch victory by dB drag racing honcho Wayne Harris.

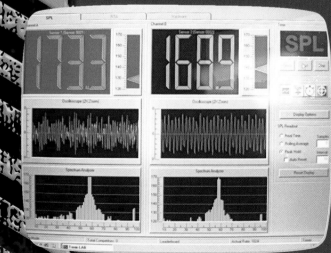

The team celebrates their world finals 173.3 dB victory.

"Basically," he continues, "I took the doors off, took the windows out, cut the whole back wall out—just took the Sawzall, went right down through the back window—cut it right through the bed, cut the B-pillars out of it, cut the wheel wells out of the bed, and then started building the framework for the doors, the new windshield, the box, the whole inside of the truck. It was a lot of fabrication.

"Take the doors, for example. When they come out of the factory," Owens says, "they're not airtight, so I built door frames with a $^1/_{16}$-inch tolerance—that's just enough room to put foam filler in and still be able to close them. Then I installed a nitrogen tank underneath that powers air rams inside the doors to shoot $^7/_8$-inch locking pins into the frame, and that sucks the doors down airtight. It would take 3,000 pounds of pressure to break that seal."

The final element to be added to the mix was something that actually had to be mixed before it could be used: concrete.

"The truck is full of concrete—there's probably 4,000 pounds in there," Owens estimates. "The back doors are full. The roof is full. Everything is full. It's actually a mortar mix that's rated at 15,000-pounds-per-square-inch at two inches thick, and I average about four to five [inches] around the whole truck. So that's where the weight comes from, that and the batteries. I could still take it out on the street and drive it, but I wouldn't want to."

As any Monster Garage machine would be, Owens's finished dB truck is up to a serious challenge—in this case, the world finals at Nashville in 2003.

Scott and his monster sound machine win their semifinal event with a 172.2 SPL dB reading. The outcome in the SPL finals is more of the same: a world record victory, with a 173.3 SPL dB score. The Owens team's first goal has been met, but the ultimate crown, for The Loudest Vehicle on the Planet, is still up for grabs. As it turns out, the spoils go to the defending champs: Team Superior and its Mad Max-style creation do it again, to the tune of 174.4 dB. It does not, as they loudly say, get ANY LOUDER THAN THAT.

At the end of the world finals, before everyone can kick back and enjoy a moment or three of uninterrupted silence, there is still one event to go, one last roar of unheard sound to crown the uncrowned king of kings: the Deathmatch Competition. Sounds deadly, and it is. Unlike the regular "soundoffs," the Deathmatch comprises what Wayne Harris calls "the most radical auto sound competition format ever devised."

Instead of a 30-second window to blast a single one- or two-second "burp" of sound, the Deathmatch competitors compete for a full, continuous 5 minutes, across which their dB levels are averaged to compute the final tally. As Wayne Harris puts it, "This event pushes system reliability right to the verge of destruction."

In the end, after five nonstop minutes of almost completely silent INCREDIBLE NOISE, Scott Owens and the F-250 emerge triumphant. They may not be the loudest vehicle on the planet—yet—but Scott is already preparing for the 2004 world finals, and if he wins there is no doubt that you will *HEAR ABOUT IT!* ◉

MONSTER MODIFIERS

HOT RODS, TUNERS, DRIFTERS, AND MORE—GREAT CUSTOMIZED
CARS AND THE PEOPLE WHO CREATED THEM

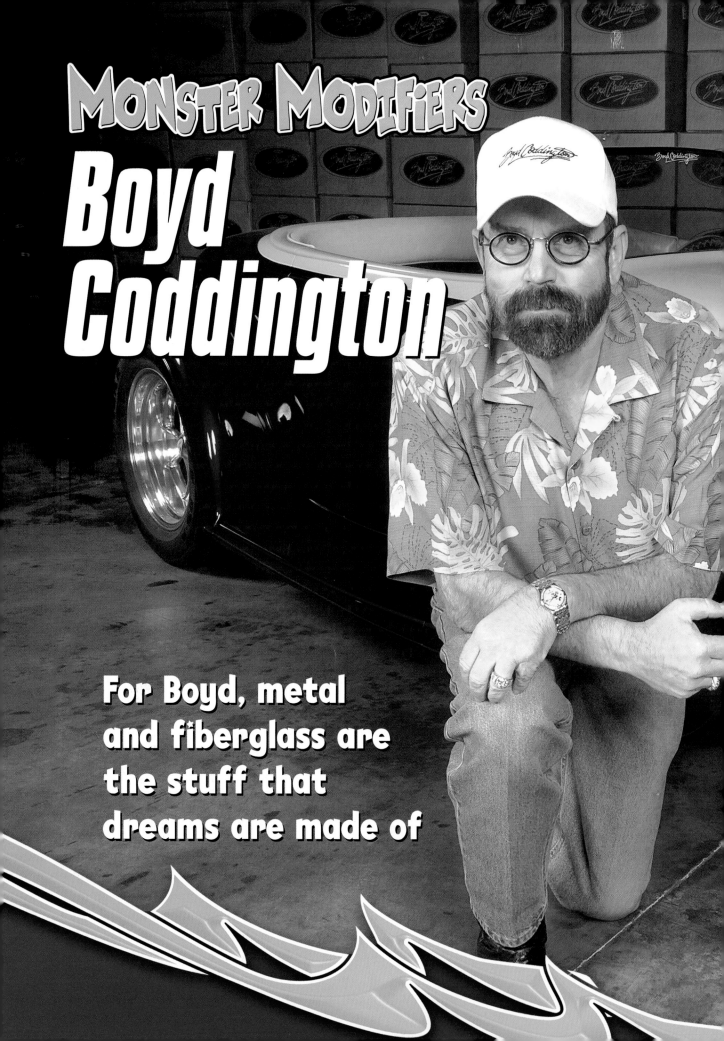

MONSTER MODIFIERS

Boyd
Coddington

For Boyd, metal
and fiberglass are
the stuff that
dreams are made of

"I think a lot of the baby boomers grew up with memories of the cars they loved in the '50s and '60s and now they are able to live their dream and drive their dream cars."
— Boyd Coddington

CadZZilla, CheZoom, The Smoothster, and The Boydster. Are they exotic cocktails at some trendy South Beach bar? MTV stars? Surfer dudes? Hot rods? Now you're getting closer. How about Hot Rods by Boyd? That's Boyd as in Boyd Coddington, a man who, over the course of his long career, has consistently stretched the boundaries of the hot rod canon.

From a 1926 Ford Tudor sedan featured in the March 1976 issue of *Street Rodder* magazine, to the latest creations being built on the Discovery Channel television series *American Hot Rod,* Coddington has managed to produce vehicles that continually blur the line between art and craft.

Born on a small Idaho farm in 1944, Boyd acquired his first car at age 13; by the time he graduated from high school he had already owned, and tinkered with, at least another half-dozen. A move to Salt Lake City in 1964 led to a three-year apprenticeship and the title of machinist.

In 1967, like so many others whose lives revolve around the automobile, he moved to Los Angeles. Married and with a growing family, he supplemented his machinist's pay with part-time work as a fabricator. Finally a job at Disneyland gave him the time and money to begin building hot rods in the garage behind his house, one of which, The Silver Bullet, won an award at the Long Beach car show. It was, according to *Street Rodder,* "The new breed of street roadster."

In 1978 he left Disney to open his own shop, where, some 26 years later, he presides over a small empire that includes not only vehicle design and fabrication but also a successful custom-wheel manufacturing facility. As the creator of the first billet aluminum wheel, Coddington's reputation as a wheel manufacturer is on a par with his hot rod rep.

In the early days of hot rodding, it was almost unheard of for someone to order up a rod to be built by someone else. Coddington, on the other hand, began doing custom work for others almost from the beginning.

"I was one of the first guys to have customers that actually paid to build cars," he says. "Vern Luce was the first customer. He liked to have me drive his car while he rode alongside on his motorcycle, so that he could see how it looked on the road. I guess that by now I've built over three hundred cars, and I still know where most of them are."

It was in the early 1980s that the first cars everyone now recognizes as having the Boyd Coddington look were built. The Coupe, in 1981, and The Roadster, in '82, set a standard in design and construction that raised the bar for every other hot rod builder. The Roadster, which won the prestigious AMBR Award (America's Most Beautiful Roadster) at the Oakland Roadster Show, cost its oilman buyer a then staggering $85,000.

The rise of these expensive contract-built rods caused a lot of grumbling, and predictions that the regular hot rod builder would be unable to compete in this new, rarefied, high-bucks world. As it turned out, the demand for custom rods has continued to grow at a rate able to support makers at all levels of the economic spectrum; and, according to Coddington, there is room at the top. "There are quite a few high-end

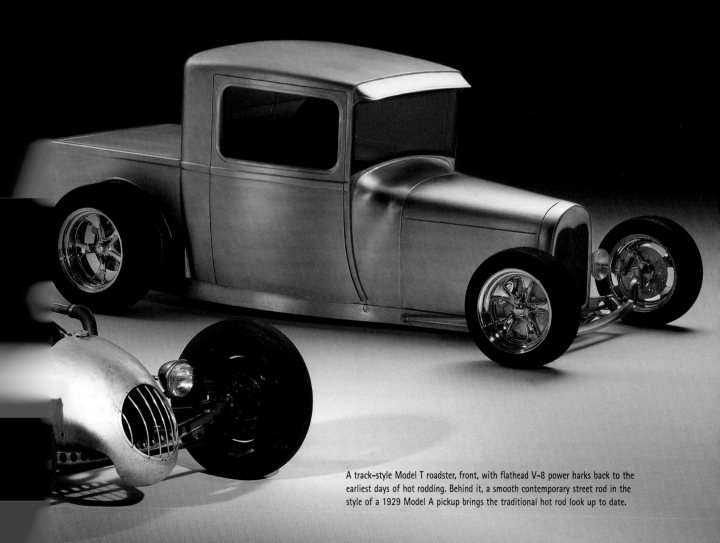

A track-style Model T roadster, front, with flathead V-8 power harks back to the earliest days of hot rodding. Behind it, a smooth contemporary street rod in the style of a 1929 Model A pickup brings the traditional hot rod look up to date.

builders today," Coddington says. "I would guess that there are probably ten or twelve at the moment. A lot of younger guys are getting into it, although not too many that are as large as we are. We employ about twenty-two people in the hot rod shop. We do everything from drawing it on paper right up to making it out of metal. We also have what we call 'photo cars,' where we've actually duplicated a couple of our real popular cars in fiberglass. We're able to send them out half-finished so the buyer can finish them off; we sell one about every two weeks. They get to select about twenty different options so they can customize it more—make it really theirs."

It would be hard to put an exact figure on the number of hot rodders that are out there in Monster Nation, but it's well above two hundred thousand (and counting). "You go to places like [the hot rod show in] Louisville, and there's thirteen or fourteen thousand cars that show up," Coddington estimates. "For the nationals in Columbus there's probably nine

thousand—that's a lot of people, and their families. We're noticing that a lot of kids are liking it as well. A lot of the response to the first *American Hot Rod* television show on Discovery was from thirteen- and fourteen-year-olds, and younger—that is really encouraging. It's now an acceptable family lifestyle. In the beginning it was such an outlaw deal, racing jalopies and all that stuff; but now you can take your five- and six-year-olds to a hot rod show and do things as a family."

The recent inclusion of hot rods at the prestigious Pebble Beach Concours d'Elegance, in a growing number of museum exhibitions, and on popular television shows, as well as Detroit-built rods like the Prowler, are all proof that the hot rod, however it evolves, is definitely here to stay.

"I think," Coddington says, "a lot of the baby boomers grew up with memories of the cars they loved in the '50s and '60s and now they are able to live their dream and drive their dream cars." ⚙

ALEX ANDERSON

Forty-year-old Alex Anderson is a custom-car builder from Long Beach, California, with certified Monster Nation credentials: He's been both a guest builder on Monster Garage and the garage manager for every build on every episode.

"A friend of mine, Brian Jendro (see page 108), from Temecula Rods and Customs, who had been on one of the first Monster Garage shows, gave them my name," he recalls. "They actually hired me to run the garage before I did the Porsche Golf Ball Collector show. I went back home and they called again to say that somebody had dropped out and they had an opening on the next show, and I went and did it. So the first week I was there, nobody knew that I was also the garage manager, and I got to find out how the shop worked without anybody really knowing what I was there to do.

"I'm responsible for everything from the tools in the shop to the parts coming into the shop. I have two hats that I wear. I wear the electrician hat and make sure all of the machines are up and running. I also wear the maintenance hat—I'm the forklift

As shop manager, it is Anderson's job to familiarize the build crews with the do's the don'ts of Monster Garage etiquette.

operator—and I do pretty much everything else in here. If something goes wrong in the shop, you'll hear my name being yelled. A lot of people turn to me for answers. So, I'm the 'go to guy,' I guess."

As a customizer and car club member, Anderson knows the sort of people who will fit in the pressure-cooker atmosphere of a Monster Garage build. He has, in fact, recommended a number of fellow customizers who have ended up on air.

"What you want are Type A people who are bossy, pushy, arrogant. We want those guys that are going to get in there and buck the system, saying 'I know what the standard way to do something is, but this is the way I do it; let's try it my way.'"

As with most of his contemporaries in the world of custom cars, Alex got his start at an early age: "I used to live down the street from a famous car painter named Pete Santini, and I'd watch him paint on my way home from junior high school. Through the school I got a job with Santini and worked there for about a year. After that I worked for Toyota for a couple of years as a mechanic, then came back to Santini and stayed until about 1986, when I went

out and worked for a number of custom shops. I worked for Colors by Dave and Fat Jack, and I painted guitars for a couple of years. Then I went to work in a machine shop and that was when I started making custom parts. When that started taking off as a side business, I decided to open my own shop, Brand X Customz. Unfortunately times got lean after 9/11. I had to close it up and get a job, and this opportunity with Monster Garage came along."

Anderson, who has customized more than one hundred cars, has a garage full of his own favorites. "I have a '99 Tacoma," he reports, "that's air-bagged and shaved; a '64 four-door Caddy with 20-inch wheels; a little Jeep that's lifted, with 31-inch Mickey Thompson tires; and my daily driver is a Camry that has three TVs in it, 19-inch wheels, and a 3,000-watt stereo system."

For Anderson, who daily commutes 160 miles round trip to work, each new Monster Garage build reminds him of the episodes that preceded it—fun, challenging, and hectic. As he puts it, in what has to be a classic understatement, "It gets a little crazy down here at times." ☼

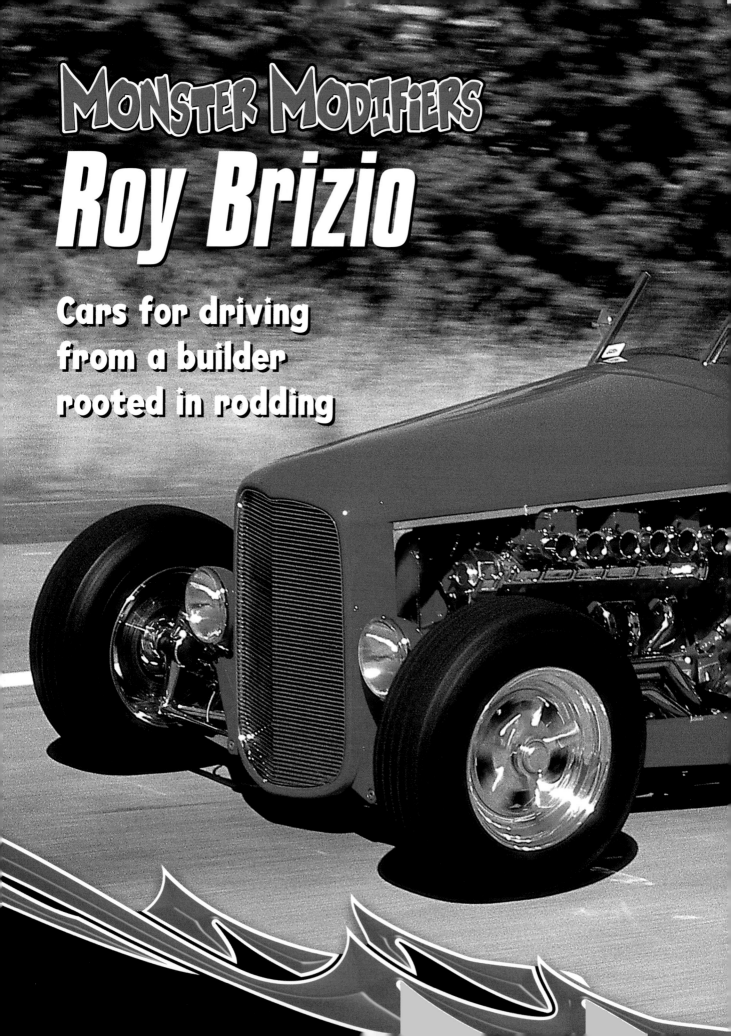

MONSTER MODIFIERS
Roy Brizio

Cars for driving from a builder rooted in rodding

" *We don't want to build show cars. Our niche is building the kinds of cars you can drive.* "
— Roy Brizio

Roy's 1932 Ford roadster with Ferrari V-12 power has covered many miles since it was named America's Most Beautiful Roadster in 1987.

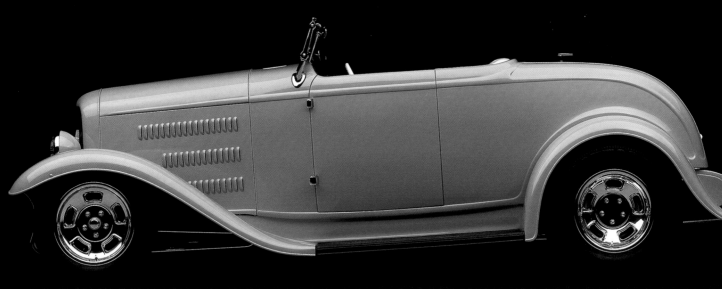

Eric Clapton's full-fendered 1932 Ford roadster has 351 Ford power, a 5-speed, and a rumble seat.

I t wasn't all that long ago that hot rods were right alongside motorcycle gangs and the red scare on the wrong end of the political correctness scale. But in less than 50 years, hot rods have emerged from the fringe into mainstream acceptance—you can tell that when a local church sponsors a car show on the lawn on a sunny Sunday afternoon. Men like Roy Brizio have helped turn that greasy garage hobby into a growing business building down-the-road hot rods for customers like Reggie Jackson, Eric Clapton, and Jeff Beck.

Roy earned his hot rod stripes as a teenager working for his father, Andy, better known as the Rodfather. Roy built inexpensive 1923 T-bucket roadster kits and worked behind the counter at his father's other business, the Champion Speed Shop in San Francisco. But before Roy turned 20, Andy sold both businesses to make custom silk-screened T-shirts. Roy's first love had always been the cars, and so, armed only with a young man's enthusiasm and hard-earned knowledge, Roy Brizio's Hot Rods opened its doors in September, 1977. That eventually grew into today's 12,000-square-foot South San Francisco enterprise with 12 employees.

Roy Brizio's greatest accomplishments include building the 1987 Oakland Roadster Show's prestigious America's Most Beautiful Roadster as well as *Hot Rod* magazine's 50th anniversary

> *We build what our customers want. As long as it's safe and doesn't look stupid, we'll build it for them.*

roadster that replicated the first *Hot Rod* magazine cover car. Other cars that Roy feels are especially significant include restoring the George Barris Ala Kart custom, and Tom McMullin's original roadster. Among the two hundred or so hot rods that have come out of Roy's shop there are eight cars for hot rod industry giant Vic Edelbrock, including the restoration of Vic, Sr.'s black '32 roadster.

The formula for Brizio's success is actually pretty simple. "We build what our customers want. As long as it's safe and doesn't look stupid," he says, "we'll build it for them." The Roy Brizio formula combines an artist's eye for the classic lines and styles of the hot rod with the journeyman's skill for building "down-the-road" machines. "We don't want to build show cars. That's not what we do here," Brizio says. He says that he has discovered that "our niche is building the kinds of cars you can drive. Over the years, these are the cars that most rodders want right now. We give 'em what they want." Business has never been better, with 25 cars currently on the waiting list to get the Brizio touch.

Brizio is also quick to acknowledge not only the skill of his 12-man crew, but also the loyalty of his customers, as reasons why Roy Brizio's Street Rods has continued to flourish. "Most of our business is return business," he says. This includes people like Vic Edelbrock, Jr., who just

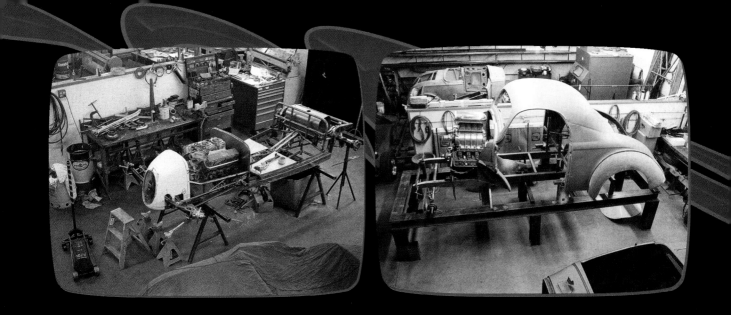

received his eighth car out of Roy's shop. And not all of these cars are '32 Fords. One particular example is a 1940 Ford coupe for rock legend Eric Clapton. The '40 is powered by a thumpin' single four-barrel 350-cubic-inch small-block Chevy with a Richmond 6-speed and a 9-inch Ford rear axle—all because Clapton likes the feel of horsepower. Brizio also added Mercedes headlights and other minor body modifications to give the classic coupe that smooth look.

But Brizio rarely strays far from the core of his business—the '32 Ford. It's one of those interesting philosophical questions to ponder: what hot rodding would look like if it weren't for the '32 Ford. Brizio is much too practical to spend much time with something as trivial as that, when there are dozens of different directions to investigate with the '32 roadster, or the three-window coupe or another of the '32's several variants. Brizio doesn't have a particular favorite, but with six '32s that are mostly

The lowboy look, with a dropped axle, channeled body, and chopped top, exemplifies early-days hot rodding.

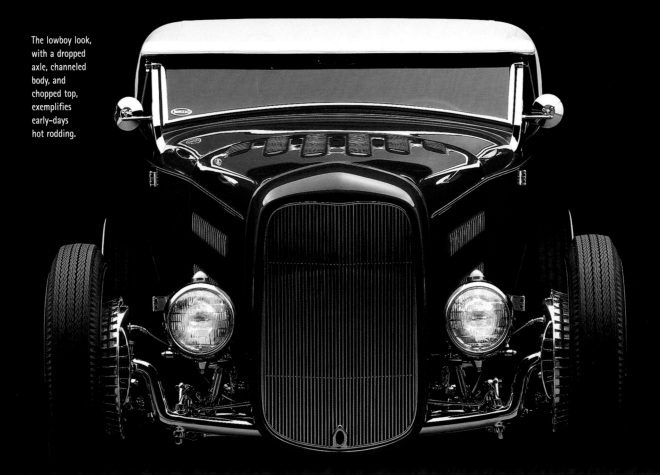

roadsters, it's clear that he has not ventured far from what most rodders feel to be the most significant car built in the 20th century.

According to Brizio, the future seems exceptionally promising for the entire hot rod industry. "There's no doubt the industry is growing," Brizio says. Thirty years ago, the fledgling fiberglass-street-rod business promised that there would always be cars to build; eventually the demand for a real steel body made the steel-body business grow, too. "Look at what Brookville is doing with those steel '32 three-window coupe bodies they make now. They've got a ton of orders for their '32 roadster with a retractable top!"

Ask any hot rodder why he built his car, and he'll tell you it's because he wanted something different. Rodders demand something that will immediately differentiate them from the dulling sameness of most new cars, with their aero-similar shapes and bland hues. While it may seem contradictory that so many hot rodders will make that claim, and then choose a '32 Ford just like everyone else, it's the specific individualizing that they do to that Ford that really counts. That's what Roy Brizio does every day. He delivers on the street rodder's need to be different, even if it's with a car that has seen the passing of over seven decades. It's still fresh and it's still fun. ◉

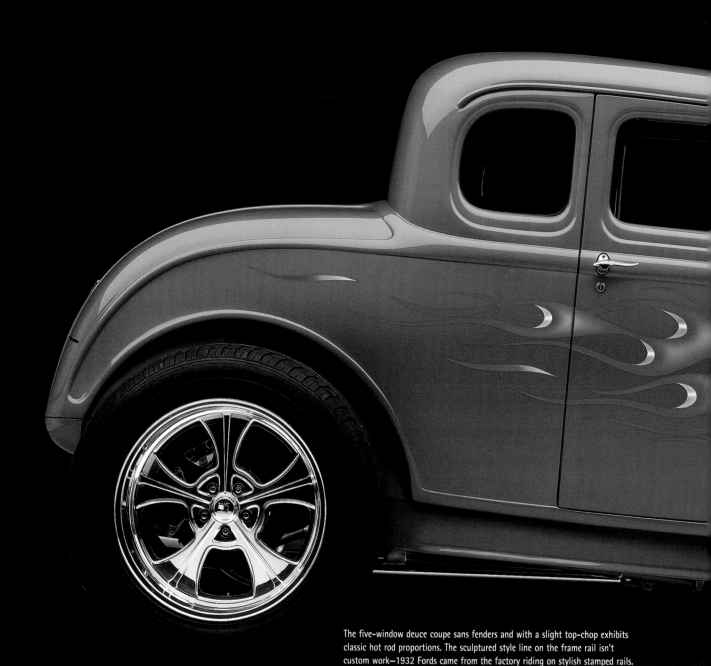

The five-window deuce coupe sans fenders and with a slight top-chop exhibits classic hot rod proportions. The sculptured style line on the frame rail isn't custom work—1932 Fords came from the factory riding on stylish stamped rails.

Roy Brizio, surrounded by works in progress, builds cars that combine classic hot rod style and attitude with modern reliability and driveability.

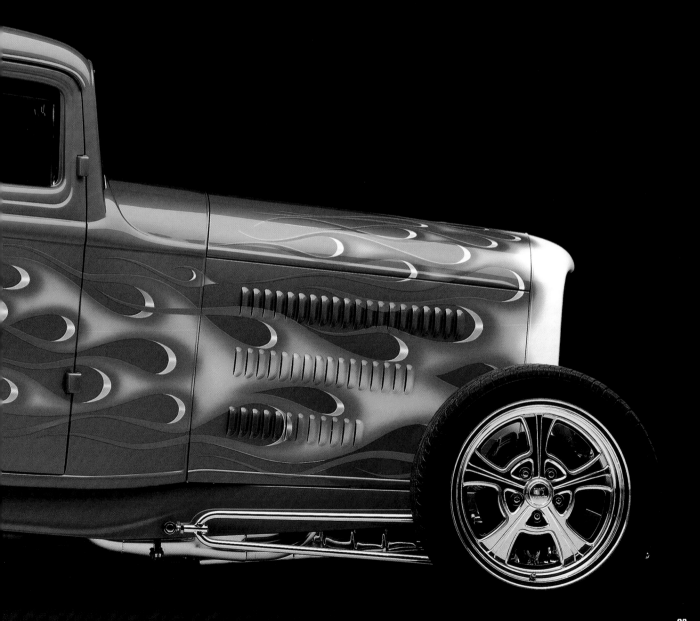

STEVE BONGE

L ike many customizers Steve Bonge has a thing for old cars with style, from 1930s hot rods up through cars of the '50s and early '60s. As he puts it, "I'm into the nostalgia thing." Bonge, who is 47, grew up on Long Island, where he first began building custom motorcycles.

"I started building bikes when I was in high school and put them in shows, and I got into cars a little bit after that," he recalls. "Most of the work I do, I do for myself. I don't want to put myself in a body shop forty hours a week."

"My main thing," he continues, "is motorcycles, and it always has been. I'm into building bikes, riding bikes, and customizing bikes. One bike I did was called the Grim Reaper. It's a 1943 Harley Davidson trike that was originally used by

Upper left: Steve Bonge and Jesse James. Upper right: Bonge at work. Lower left: Bonge, with glasses, left, Jesse, and others from the Hot Dogster crew gearing up for the Letterman show. Lower right: Bonge, right, and well-known bike builder Indian Larry as they work on the Hot Dogster.

meter maids to hand out traffic tickets. I extended the front end, molded in an upside down Sportster tank, painted it metal-flake green—my first paint job—and then I took another Harley Davidson rear and attached it to a coffin with a trailer hitch so I could hook it onto the back of the trike. I used to put it in various car shows. It was a pretty radical bike for back in the '70s."

Bonge also was part of the Monster Garage build crew for the Hot Dogster episode that was featured on the David Letterman show. Bonge was there when Jesse James took the Dogster for some trial runs down 53rd Street in New York City.

"Jesse did about three or four passes with it down 53rd Street and was barely able to stop before he hit 10th Avenue. We had a permit to do it, but the cops made a call to the mayor's office and they pulled the permit—nonnegotiable, that's it. Doing the show was fun. I'm really lucky that Jesse asked me to do it." ◎

From 1978, Bonge and his Grim Reaper trike.

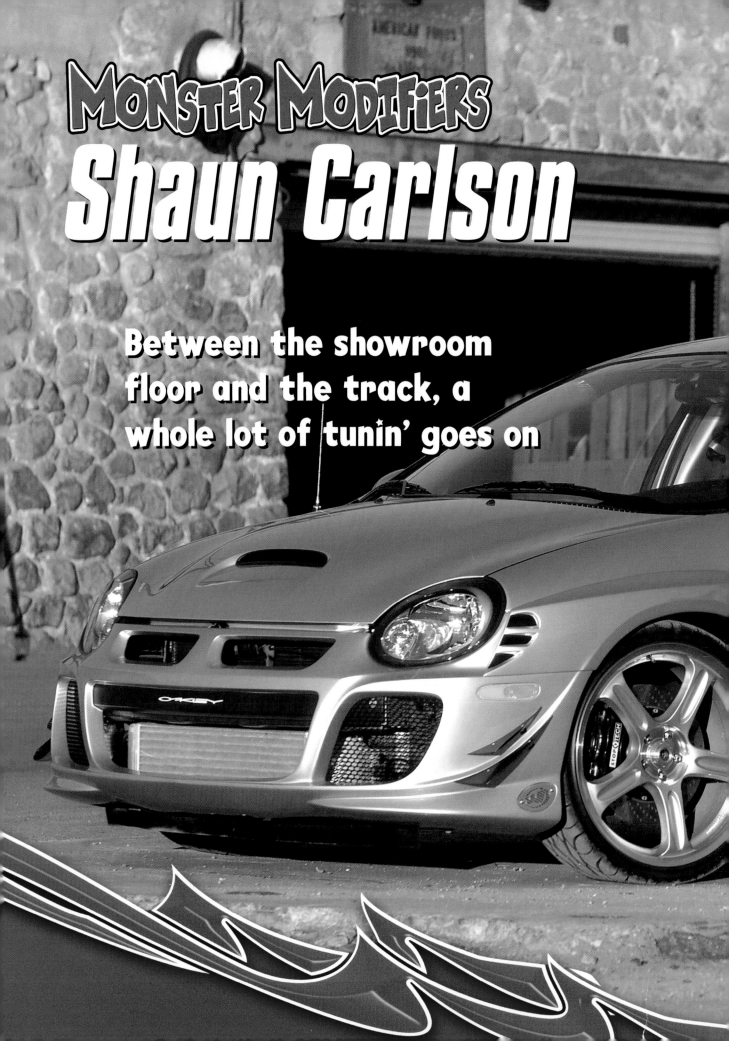

MONSTER MODIFIERS
Shaun Carlson

Between the showroom
floor and the track, a
whole lot of tunin' goes on

"What we're doing now is no different than what all the hot rodders did years ago. We're just the next hot rod generation."
— Shaun Carlson

Shaun Carlson, right, and fellow tuner Rob Miller with a tricked out Dodge SRT-4.

T hey're fast! They're furious! They sound like a hive of large, angry bees. They're high-revving tuners, and if you haven't heard them buzzing around the neighborhood, turn on your hearing aid.

There is some dispute as to when the tuner revolution arrived on our shores. The Petersen Automotive Museum in Los Angeles credits the Datsun 510, which became a winner on the tracks back in the 1960s. Datsun dealers began offering aftermarket performance parts to the public, creating what the museum calls "the first true Tuner Car." Others point to the introduction of the Honda Civic in 1973 and the slow but steady rise of aftermarket add-ons for the little pocket rocket.

Initially confined to the Los Angeles area, tuners began to move into the cultural mainstream in the early 1990s. Whatever the time line, there is no dispute that today tuners can be found wherever the rubber meets the road. The tuner car craze has obvious parallels with the hot rod scene back in the late '40s and early '50s. The market is fueled mostly by young men driving small, inexpensive, often secondhand cars that are customized with all the accessories that credit can buy: skirts, spoilers, L.E.D. lights, carbon-fiber panels, nitrous oxide bottles, custom wheels, turbochargers, and stereo systems. All of these can easily cost more than the sticker price for the vehicle. Tuner car drivers, like their hot rod predecessors, often find themselves at odds with the police, as street racing is not exactly uncommon. And while the drive-in movie theaters may be gone, the ghosts of *Hot Rod Girl* and *Dragstrip Riot* live on in films like *The Fast and the Furious* and *2 Fast, 2 Furious.*

In 1997, aftermarket tuner equipment sales reached about $295 million. By 2003 the figure had soared to $2.2 billion—the fastest growing segment of the $27 billion automotive aftermarket business. If one event was the starting point for the current tuner craze, it probably would be the first Hot Import Nights show in Long Beach, California, in 1998. Now nationwide, Hot Import Nights are attended not only by the young tuner crowd, but also by major automakers looking for the next trend to incorporate into their factory-built vehicles.

The tuner market can be divided into several categories, including: street, show, sound, and strip (which is experiencing the fastest growth). It was the National Hot Rod Association (NHRA) that earlier took hot rods off the street and into the regulated environment of the sanctioned drag strip. The same thing is happening today with tuners. One man who has been there pretty much from the beginning is 29-year-old Californian Shaun Carlson.

"When my generation," says Carlson, "was between 13 and 16, all of our brothers or people that we knew had Mustangs and Camaros, that was the cool thing. A lot of the cars that the 16-year-olds were getting were family hand-me-downs—a lot of Hondas, because they were reliable and got good gas mileage. No one thought they would become performance-oriented. Well, as soon as we got those Hondas we'd go to the street races to hang out. We got so tired of having all these Camaro and Mustang guys making fun of us that we just started fixing up the Hondas to beat them. Then it just sort of took off and the Honda Civic kind of turned into the Mustang or Camaro, or the '57 Chevy of its time—the mainstream car. What we're doing now is no different than what all the hot rodders did years ago. We're just the next hot rod generation."

It soon became obvious that the crowds of kids who were hanging out and racing their Hondas or other small imports on the streets could just as easily be moved to the track.

"The first person to really bring street racing to the track," according to Carlson, "was a guy named Frank Choy. He had what was called 'The Battle of the Imports.' It was held in Palmdale, California. First it was once a year, then twice, then finally I think it was four times. Frank would pull in thousands of cars—it just grew huge. To kind of jump ahead, I think this year alone there were over 500 events during the summer that had to do with compact shows and races. It's going to get bigger and bigger.

"The Ford Focus was the first domestic manufacturer to come into the market. They realized they needed to embrace the aftermarket because that's pretty much what controls new car sales. When Dodge was developing the SRT-4, they actually went out and saw what the kids were doing—what they wanted, what kind of intercooler, tire package, wheel size. Instead of coming out with a car that everyone's going to rip everything off and throw in the trash, they offered all the extra stuff right on the car. Mopar's been working with the aftermarket companies and putting their equipment on when the car is built."

For Carlson, one of the stars of the sport-compact drag racing world, the tuner revolution has proven to be the ultimate combination of fun and success. His company, NuFormz, in Ontario, California, makes performance parts for the import industry as well as for the Dodge SRT-4.

"My life is my racecar, my business, the shop, and my girlfriend," Shaun Carlson says. "It's been great. I believe that if you want something bad enough and stick with it, you'll get it. I've worked my butt off. I'm no different than anyone else—anyone else who's gone out, had a goal, and worked for it. I never thought it was going to take me as far as it has in my life." ◎

Tuners are accessorized front and back, under the hood, behind the wheel, and anyplace else the producers of aftermarket add-ons can fit a custom detail. Some of the additions such as custom rims or skirts are mostly cosmetic. But some, like a turbocharger and other high-performance engine upgrades, turn a nice little car into a racing machine.

MONSTER MODIFIERS
Calvin Wan

Drifting along like a roaring, tire-smoking, side-sliding tumbleweed

" I believe drifting will
become a major segment
of motorsport in America. "
— Calvin Wan

In the early 1990s young Americans began learning about drifting (see "Drift Racing," opposite page) through Japanese magazines and videos. Before long they were drifting their Corollas and RX-7s along the canyon roads of Central and Southern California. Some early drifters, wanting to get off the streets into a safer environment, tried hooking up with established sanctioning bodies. But "grip drivers"—the drifters' term for most other types of racers—and drifters mixed like oil and water. This led to the formation of an umbrella organization, the Drift Association, and events like Drift Days (held at assorted California speedways), the RSR Drift Festival, and the Falken Drift Showoff.

By 2003 there was a fan base strong enough to buy ten thousand tickets to the first D1 Grand Prix at California's Irwindale Speedway. And there were U.S.-born racers: eight of the 27 entrants in the event were Americans. These drivers were selected based upon their showing at a preliminary event earlier that year where the top 50 U.S. drifters were judged by a team of Japanese experts. It remained to be seen how the Americans would stack up against the more experienced Japanese drifters.

Calvin Wan, a 26-year-old San Franciscan, was one of the Americans. "I've been fascinated with cars for as long as I can remember," Wan says. "Even before I could read I was already looking at pictures of cars in magazines and brochures. Over the years I've had many auto-related jobs, such as

installing tires and working as a valet-parking trainer for a hotel in San Francisco. My family never really approved of my addiction to cars, so I pretty much did everything car-related on my own. In June of 1998 I cofounded Graphtech Graphics, which specializes in vehicle graphics and decals."

Wan's first look at drifting came from imported videos in the early 1990s. "When I first started driving," he recalls, "I was mainly into drag racing, but I would mess around from time to time doing a lot of e-brake turns everywhere. That got me into sanctioned autocross competitions. I drifted every now and then, but I was mainly concentrating on grip driving—I also did a lot of canyon driving. In November 2002, I got a chance to drift in an organized environment at Speedtrial USA; from then on my focus shifted to drifting. I became a drift instructor for Drift Association/Club 4ag and the Nor Cal Drift Association, and I attended every drift event on the West Coast in 2003."

For the D1 event, Wan's Falken-sponsored red Mazda FD3S RX-7 featured an A'pex N1 damper-system coilover suspension, A'pex GT-spec exhaust, gold Gram Lights wheels, and an A'pex power FC engine controller. Unfortunately, one item he hadn't added was the full roll cage mandated by the D1 rules. Wan and most of the Americans learned about the rule just a few days before the event. Wan borrowed a roll cage at the last minute, and, as it turned out, the cage came in pretty handy—he tagged the wall twice. The first was just your average 40 miles per hour drift into a retaining wall during a practice run. It caused enough suspension damage to hamper the car's performance, but not enough to keep him out of his competition runs later that day. After readjusting the camber to at least approximate the original settings, Wan headed back into competition. That's when the real trouble hit, and hit is the operative word. "Driving the car back to the staging area," he recalls, "I knew it was in bad shape, but there was no turning back."

The competition consisted of three solo runs, with judges choosing the best of the three. A good score was needed to move on into the next round. On the first two runs the damaged suspension prevented the car from sustaining its drifts; on the third run, Wan decided to go for broke. He floored it and held his drift through the outer oval, but his speed put him off line for the next turn. "I flicked it back hard to the left to dive into the inner oval," he says, "but the speed was too fast and the car just spun around and slammed into the cement barrier while the car was deep in third gear. The hit was pretty violent. Once the car settled down I looked around and everything seemed OK, so I started it back up and I heard a tremendous roar from the crowd as I waved and drove off back to the pits."

Wan had hit the wall at about 70 and came close to leaping over it. He emerged unscathed but the RX-7 was done for the day. The battle for top honors came down to two top Japanese stars, 2002 D1 Drift Champion Katsuhiro Ueo and Nobutero Taniguchi. The battle between Ueo's Toyota Corolla/Trueno AE86 and Taniguchi's Nissan Silva S15 was so exciting that when it was all over the fans began to chant, "One more time. One more time." The pair obliged with a final round of screaming, smoking, rubber-ripping drifts. Ueo won when Taniguchi spun and kissed the wall.

In 2004 the Sports Car Club of America (SCCA) will run a four-round drift championship, with the winner getting to compete in the D1 Grand Prix Championship Finals in Japan. Wan plans to run. "I believe drifting will become a major segment of motorsport in America," he says. "Many companies, including major auto manufacturers, are getting involved, and even people without performance driving experience are willing to get into a rear-drive car and try drifting to see what all the fuss is about. I think drifting is here to stay in America." ◉

DRIFT RACING

About 15 years ago Japanese *hashiriya*, or street racers, discovered that driving their cars in controlled drifts—or slides—called *choku-dori* at relatively low velocity produced enough noise, tire smoke, and excitement to satisfy all but the most jaded racing fans. They also took note of the fact that the police were much less likely to arrest them for it than for drag racing. Thus was born drifting.

As with any automotive activity involving young people with disposable income, aftermarket manufacturers quickly developed products to aid the quest for sideways thrills. Drifting grew rapidly underground. Then, with support from manufacturers and the media, it grew into a sport so popular that top Japanese drivers became something akin to rock stars. Drifting came of age in the United States on August 31, 2003, with the running of the first D1 Grand Prix in America at Southern California's Irwindale Speedway.

Drifting may prove to be the next big thing for the import tuner market, as important as sport compact drag racing. If not, as *Autoweek* magazine puts it, "It's at least the next small or medium thing."

Nick Fousekis, a marketing manager for Falken tires, has no doubts about the appeal and staying power of drifting. "I feel it's the next step in entertainment-and-motorsport combination-type events," he says. "It's a great equalizer in that you don't need four, five, six hundred horsepower to go out and put on a great show and really get the crowd riled up. It's based more on the setup of your vehicle and the driver's skill, in comparison with a lot of other types of events. You can drift a bone-stock rear-wheel-drive car. A lot of the '80s Corollas only have 110 to 120 horsepower, and yet they make great drifting machines. It's a sport where the little guy has a chance against the big guys."

LISA LEGOHN

For Lisa Legohn, a crew member on the Limousine Fire Truck build, the journey to Monster Garage and Monster Nation began when she was in high school. "I was 17 years old and going to Hollywood High when I heard about this regional occupational program that taught welding, and I said, 'What is welding?' A counselor—I don't think she knew—said it's 'like fire and a helmet,' and I said, jokingly, 'Send me there. My mom ought to get a kick out of this.'"

"I went to the class," she remembers, "and there's all these young African-American guys; and it was me and three other females with all these guys, and it was like, 'Whoa!' We made a pact that we would stay, and three of the four of us did."

As it turned out, welding was just a tiny bit different from what Lisa had had in mind when she signed up for the course. "I remember lighting the torch for the first time," she says. "It went 'pop-pop,' and I threw it one way and started running the other way. I literally ran about a block; but the instructor got me to come back and try it again."

"So I took the bus from Hollywood to Watts every Saturday from eight to three," Legohn recalls. "It started out as a joke, but I really liked it. The whole aura of welding captivated me. I was just fascinated with the things you could do with steel. I knew then that I was going to be a welder."

Years of working on various manufacturing and construction sites made Legohn realize that

Lisa Legohn, Jesse James, and the rest of the crew at work on the world's most elegant fire truck.

she couldn't spend the rest of her life doing that sort of heavy work. She says, "I thought, 'When I get older, how am I going to do this?' Men and women do have different physical characteristics, and this type of work takes a toll on you as a female. And then, when you get off work and you plan on a date, you go through this whole metamorphosis because you're a mess." Her solution to the problem was to take all that she had learned over the years and put it to use by becoming a teacher herself. Now she teaches welding at Los Angeles Trade Technical College. Among her many pupils, at least one, Renee Newell, has appeared as a builder on Monster Garage, in the Chevy Impala Zamboni episode.

A single parent with a teenage daughter, Lisa is a cancer survivor who has been in remission for more than three years. According to her doctors, her strong physical condition and tough mental attitude contributed to her recovery.

"I said to myself, 'I'm gonna make it; I'm gonna beat this.' I missed work two months," she says, "and when I went back I gave up my night job. I'd been teaching part-time at Compton College for twenty years. For a while I tried to do both, and people said, 'Why are you doing this?' And I said, 'If I don't, I'll lay down and die. I have to fight.'"

"I go to my oncologist every three months to get my blood checked, and it gets a little scary sometimes," says Legohn. "I guess that's why I'm so loquacious now—I never used to say anything, I was very shy, but now I let it out. I've learned a lot from this."

Legohn, who got plenty of Monster Nation street cred when Jesse James called her a "real welder," was asked to appear on a second Monster Garage episode. Because of her teaching schedule she had to decline, but that doesn't mean she wouldn't like to come back.

"I had a lot of fun doing the show," she says, "and I'd love to do another one." ⚙

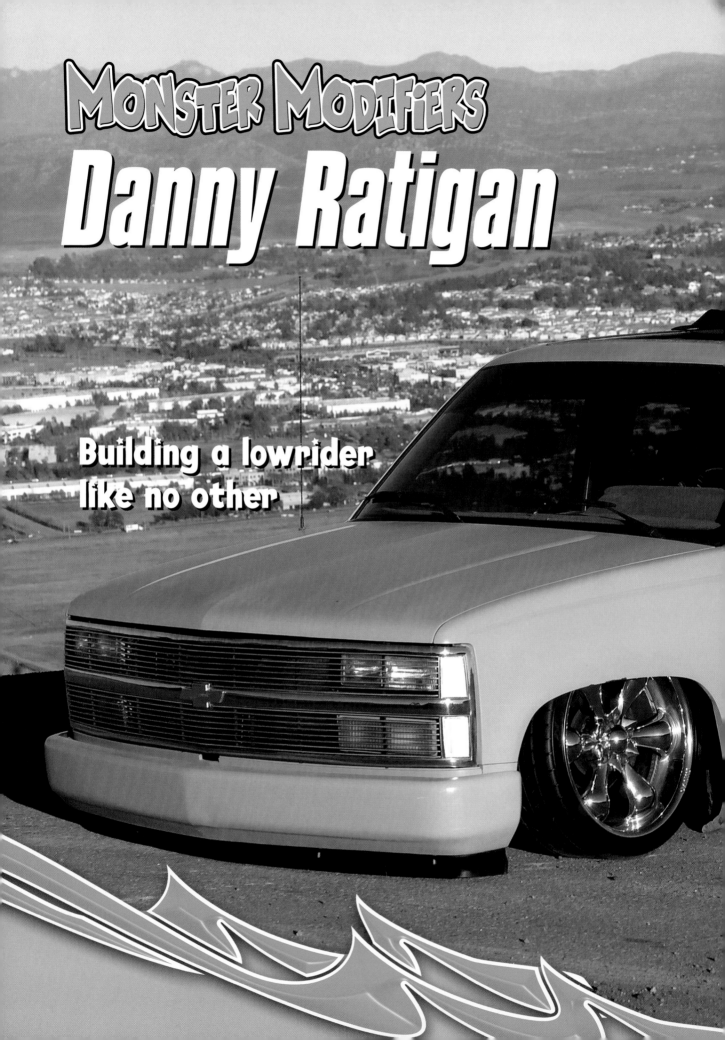

MONSTER MODIFIERS
Danny Ratigan

**Building a lowrider
like no other**

"I can weld, I can do bodywork, I can cut and grind—anything I can reach I can do myself."
— Danny Ratigan

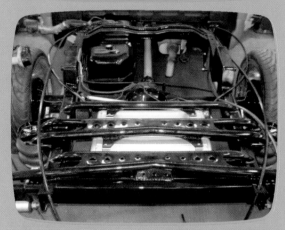

Brian Jendro and some of his handiwork. The hand controls allow Ratigan to operate the truck without relying on the pedals.

anny Ratigan, a 23-year-old gearhead from Vista, California, drives a 1993 Chevy Silverado lowrider pickup. He and the crew at Temecula Rods and Customs outfitted and customized the truck over an eight-month period. The pickup has all of the usual lowrider stuff, including an air-bag suspension system, shaved door handles, flared bedsides, and custom wheels. But it also has features not usually found in even the most extreme lowriders: hand-operated controls.

Ratigan, who currently works in the construction business, has been a paraplegic for the past ten years. "I was riding in a car when I was 13 years old," he says. "We got hit by another car and the impact busted my aorta. They had to do heart bypass surgery to bring me back to life, but the surgery took so long that some of the nerves in my spinal cord died and I lost the use of my legs. I was in the hospital about four months with therapy and everything. About a month after I got out, I adapted my quad so I could ride it, and I went back to desert off-roading. After doing that a bit, going way too fast, I wised up. So I got a buggy that a few friends and I fixed up with hand controls. After that I went to an off-road truck with a full roll cage, off-road suspension, and everything."

Ratigan's desire to modify his vehicles began with the first one he owned, a VW bus that he lowered and otherwise customized to the extent that his wallet would allow. In the ensuing years he has kept true to that philosophy, building cars and trucks that he drives until he feels it's time to move on and build another one. Although he's taken the Silverado to some of the Southern California car shows, it is, as are all of his vehicles, a daily driver and not, as he puts it, "a trailer queen."

"I'm into old cars too," he says. "I just got rid of a 1961 Ford Galaxy that we air-bagged and did a bunch of motor work on; now I'm just getting started on a 1950 Ford shoebox. I can weld, I can do bodywork, I can cut and grind—anything I can reach I can do myself. I have all of the tools and equipment for that. But for things where you need two arms and two legs to roll around under the car or whatever, that's when places like Temecula Rods and Customs come in handy."

Ratigan's current ride, the '93 Chevy lowrider pickup pictured on the previous two pages, features front, back, and side-to-side air-bag suspension created by Brian Jendro of Temecula Rods. The rear suspension is a custom-made cantilever with a 12-inch lift. Air management is handled by three Thomas 317 compressors with two five-gallon tanks.

Builders Brian Jendro, Matt East, and Sal Marchese, rear, and Danny Ratigan, front, meet in the Temecula Rods and Customs shop in Temecula, California.

The truck's low, lean, graceful look comes from its full phantom front grille, a smoothed front bumper, a shaved and extended tailgate, and a 2½-inch body drop. A 40-by-40-inch Britex sliding rag top lets in the Southern California rays.

While Ratigan's situation and his response to it may seem unique, there are others he has met who face similar challenges, and whose "get on with it" attitudes are much like his.

"There's a guy named Steve," he says, "who goes to a lot of car shows. He has a Dodge Ram that's on 22s and has air bags and a custom stereo system—it's a neat-looking truck. Now he's trying to come up with his own custom wheels for wheelchairs. He has a set of prototype wheelchair wheels that Oasis made for him that actually match the ones on his truck—and on my truck too. It's pretty cool."

While it's true that Ratigan and other modifiers in similar situations work on their vehicles in much the same way that Jesse James, or any other rod builder, does, they do encounter some problems not faced by their compatriots. "I was working on this part," Ratigan recalls, "when I started feeling something funny, so I backed up out from under the work table, looked down, and it was like, 'Oh God. There's some flame here.' My leg was on fire—talk about hot wheels, that was crazy."

He'd probably be the last to admit it, but of all the rodders, customizers, and other assorted auto modifiers inhabiting this Monster Nation of ours, Danny Ratigan is one cool dude. ☯

MONSTER MODIFIERS
Lenny Gruver

Thirty-six-year-old Lenny Gruver lives in that famous hotbed of hot rodding, Kinsman, Ohio—about fifty miles east of Cleveland. In his words, "The street rodding scene is *obscene* around my area. There's nowhere that you can go that you can't talk to somebody that owns a machine shop where you can get something done—mostly the old-style stuff. You couldn't believe the influence of street rods that I have seen in my area—and a lot of them are daily drivers. We have supposedly the biggest concentration of hot rods in the world here in northeastern Ohio."

Five days a week Gruver puts in his forty hours for General Motors. But in his off time he's the proprietor of Gruvy's House of Hack, a Monster Nation moniker if ever there was one.

"I do everything and anything you want: hydraulics, air, suicide doors, body drops—stuff like that. But," he says, "with the forty hours a week working on the other job, it gets tough."

Like most hot rodders, Gruver got the bug at an early age, in his case from his father. "He took me to car shows," Gruver recalls, "before I even knew what was going on. He bought my first vehicle, a 1969 Camaro, when I was about fourteen. I worked on it with him for two years, and the day I got my driver's license I had a full-show Camaro to drive to school. It was insane. He's a good dude."

In 2003 Gruver brought one of his creations (pictured, left) to the SEMA (Specialty Equipment Market Association) show in Las Vegas, and it drew quite a crowd to its assigned space just outside one of the main exhibition halls. It began life as a 1989 Chevy S-10 Extended Cab, but it has ended up pure Gruver. It features, says Gruver, "a 310-horsepower, 2.5-litre Pontiac motor. The interior," he adds, "is leather and ostrich skin with a German square-weave rug."

"I bought it brand new to cut it up," Gruver recalls. "I drove it two miles from the dealer and the very next weekend I lowered it. Then about every six months for the next five years I did something different to it. I got into the real customizing when I got a little closer to paying it off—did all the normal lowrider stuff. Just worked on it year after year. I'm hoping it's a good representation of the old and the new. I'm trying to give a little bit back to the people that really started this stuff." ◉

" I do everything and anything you want: hydraulics, air, suicide doors, body drops—stuff like that. "
— Lenny Gruver

MONSTER MODIFIERS
Double Down Club

N ew Year's Eve is a time for making plans and resolutions, even though they are often forgotten as soon as the celebrations are over. At a New Year's party two years ago, one group of guys in Southern California hatched a plan to form a lowrider club in which all of the vehicles would be "dually" pickup trucks—the big ones with dual rear wheels. They not only made it happen, says club president Jose Rodriguez, they did it within a week.

"The very next weekend the Double Down Club was formed. We wanted to be different so we decided to make the club for duallies only. We are a family-oriented club made up of close friends and family members who like to have picnics and go to car shows and cruise nights. We now have a total of 11 active members, and all of us own duallies."

The Double Down trucks are customized according to each member's own taste and budget. All are

Chevy or GMC trucks, with some featuring Escalade front ends and others sporting the Denali nose. Their suspension systems are either air-bag or hydraulic, and the interiors are outfitted with custom upholstery, high-end stereo systems, and multiple in-car TV monitors. Members are constantly working on the trucks, making both cosmetic and mechanical improvements. "We take pride in our duallies and like to show them off," says Rodriguez. "There's nothing like the feeling when we all roll up at a show or cruise night, hitting our switches, and watching everyone turn to look at our train of duallies, and seeing the expressions on their faces."

While the Double Down Club may be somewhat unconventional in its choice of vehicles, its members are all proud to be a part of the lowrider culture, a tradition whose roots in Southern California go back more than fifty years. ◉

"There's nothing like the feeling when we all roll up, hitting our switches, watching everyone turn to look at our train of duallies, and seeing the expressions on their faces."
– Jose Rodriguez

MONSTER PLANET
THE DESIGNERS

Franco Sbarro

Francesco Zefferino Sbarro was born in Apulia, Italy, in 1939. At 18 he left Italy for Switzerland, where he quickly found work as a mechanic. Within two years he had opened a small shop where he specialized in repairing Borgwards and BMWs. His big break came when he became chief mechanic for the Filipinetti racing team's Ford GT-40s. He then made the transition from mechanic to constructor with replica GT-40 and Lola T70 racers and a modified VW Karmann Ghia called the Coupe Filipinetti.

Encouraged by this success, Sbarro left Filipinetti in 1968 and founded his own company, the Atelier de Construction Automobile (ACA). His first independent creation, the Dominique III, a small sports car with a giant rear spoiler, gained enough attention and sales to ensure his future as a designer and builder of highly individualized vehicles.

The fact that he has had no formal design training, nor an engineering degree, has had little effect on Sbarro's ability to attract private and corporate customers for his unique creations.

He also has created two design schools, one in France and one in Morocco, where students must create their own vehicles from concept to road test in order to graduate.

Sbarro has created more than 100 one-of-a-kind cars that have been featured at major auto shows worldwide. Asked why he designs such unusual vehicles, his charming reply was, "If we all like the same woman, we have a problem." ◉

Top of page: This 4WD was built on a Range Rover chassis and is powered by a 350-horsepower, 6.4-litre Mercedes Benz engine. Conceived for desert racing, it features a Kevlar body, wheels adapted from a Boeing 747 main landing gear, an electric generator, and a mini-motorbike in case you find yourself stranded in the dunes of the Sahara. Above: This 30-foot-long combination monster truck and top-fuel dragster is powered by a 1,500-horsepower, 27.5-litre Merlin V-12 aircraft engine. At five tons and with seating for five, it needs a lot of power. It even does wheelies, sort of. The front suspension is designed to allow the nose to shoot skyward without the front wheels ever leaving the ground. This is a car Jesse James could love.

Luigi Colani

Luigi Colani, who was called the "Leonardo Da Vinci of the 20th Century" by Germany's *Stern* magazine, was born in Berlin in 1928. After growing up in a household where he and his three siblings were encouraged by their parents to design and make their own toys, Colani became an art student at Berlin's Academy of Fine Arts. He next studied aerodynamics at the University of Paris, where, on the side, he developed expertise in car design, racecar development, and fiberglass-body manufacturing techniques.

His first prominent design success came in 1954, when he won the Golden Rose Award for a sports coupe based on the Fiat 1100. This was followed by a famous fiberglass kit car, the Colani GT Spyder. He has since gone on to design some of the wildest and best-known concept cars and trucks in the world.

Looking like some giant prehistoric insect, the Colani supersemi can be found roaming the autoroutes of Europe.

Colani's signature look, whether on small objects he has designed, such as stereo headphones, or large ones, such as the windshield and leading edges of the truck pictured above, is roundedness, with an emphasis on comfortable ergonomics and smooth aerodynamics. ◉

Left: The Rinspeed Presto, which telescopes to a smaller size for tight parking. Right: The Rinspeed X-Trem Multi Utility Vehicle (MUV), which comes with a mini-hovercraft.

Frank Rinderknecht

Frank Rinderknecht, CEO of Rinspeed Design near Zurich, Switzerland, founded the company when he was just 23 years old. In the ensuing 25 years he has built, modified, or customized upwards of 100 cars per year at his shop, designed and built numerous concept cars, and worked as a tuner of high-end sports cars like Mercedes Benz and Porsche. He's also a major manufacturer of aftermarket wheels. Rinderknecht also does custom work on helicopters and boats, and sells his patented X-Tra-Lift, a device that sits in the bed of a pickup and has the ability to lift up to 1,320 pounds. Not bad for a guy who started out as an installer of sunroofs.

At 19, Rinderknecht was in Los Angeles working for a company that did van conversions, often including sunroofs. When he returned to Switzerland in 1977, he set up shop installing sunroofs that he imported from California. The business was so successful that he was able to found Rinspeed.

The aftermarket wheels, accessories, tuners and conversions may pay the bills, but it is the concept cars that get the attention. As Rinderknecht puts it, "These cars are all of our publicity money for the year, concentrated." One has only to look at them to understand why. ◉

MONSTER ART CARS

DON'T PUT THESE AMAZING WORKS OF ART IN A MUSEUM—THEY LOOK MUCH BETTER ON THE ROAD

MONSTER ART CARS

HARROD BLANK

The Art Car artist who encourages and documents other Art Car artists

"*An art car expresses the ideas, values, and dreams of an individual. There are no rules for making one, and no boundaries or guidelines to follow.*"
— HARROD BLANK

Harrod Blank in his Camera Van, with its more than two thousand cameras and an equal number of flash cubes.

Harrod Blank, the man whose name has become almost synonymous with the term *art car*, was born in Westminster, California, in 1963. He was surrounded by art and artists from an early age. Both his father, Les, an internationally known filmmaker, and his mother, Gail, a ceramicist, were talented and highly individualistic—two traits that son Harrod seems to have assimilated completely. At the age of six, after the family relocated to the Santa Cruz Mountains, Harrod developed, as he puts it, "a feeling of alienation from people." Yet he had a strong desire to stand out among his peers, somehow or other. As it turned out, the means to accomplish that came with his learner's permit. Getting a driver's license is a major rite of passage for any teenager, but for Harrod Blank it was even more so.

"When it came time to drive," he recalls, "my life changed drastically. I bought a 1965 all-white VW Bug. I drove it around, but it was the most boring car in the world. I felt I had to show people I wasn't just like everyone else, that I wasn't just another VW Bug driver, but that I was Me. This desire to show my individuality, and to create my own car, would become the foundation of my whole career."

Influenced by readings in Native American philosophy, and by the Jamaican

> **"** *By the time I entered college, I had a reputation for being the guy who drove that crazy car.* **"**

film *The Harder They Fall*, starring Jimmy Cliff, Blank and a friend spray-painted the car with pictures of musician Bob Marley and other reggae-themed scenes and christened it the Rasta Bug.

"By the time I entered college in 1981," he says, "I had a reputation for being the guy who drove that crazy car." In 1984, while a student at the University of California at Santa Cruz, Blank went to Mexico City for a year of study. When he returned to the U.S. he began repainting the Bug with bright, gaudy colors, and he added objects like bones, trophies, and, as a hood ornament, a globe. The Bug was beginning to morph into something else— but what?

"One day," says Blank, "my friend Kevin and I were sitting in the car when several tourists came up and they all said, 'Oh, my God, what is this?' Kevin said, 'That's what you should call the car, *Oh My God!* I agreed, and the name has stuck ever since."

Blank has gone on to conceive and construct two more art cars, Camera Van and Pico de Gallo. More widely, his dedication to the art car has resulted in recognition and respectability for the art car movement. In 2002 he was guest curator of a major art car exhibition at the Petersen Automotive Museum in Los Angeles. His art car documentaries, *Wild Wheels* and *Driving the Dream,* were

Harrod Blank's Pico de Gallo is an "interactive music mobile" that he created in 1988. "It was my third art car," he says, "and its name is Spanish for a spicy salsa or hot sauce. My fantasy was to make a performance vehicle for a mariachi, harking back to the year I spent in Mexico City."

broadcast on national television. He's the co-producer of one of the most important social dates on the Monster Nation calendar, the annual ArtCar Fest (held in various locations in the San Francisco Bay Area). The films, the exhibitions and festivals, as well as his books, *Wild Wheels* and *Art Cars,* have inspired many others to see their cars as something other than a way to get to the mall.

What exactly is an art car, and is it art? Artists were using the automobile as a canvas as far back as the 1920s, when Sonia Delaunay painted cars with colorful geometric designs that were based on her paintings of the period. Working with the French auto manufacturers Talbot and Citroen, she coordinated these cars with a line of women's clothing that featured the same color principles. In the 1970s and '80s, BMW commissioned artists like Andy Warhol, Frank Stella, Roy Lichtenstein, and Alexander Calder to paint cars that were then raced at the 24 Hours of Le Mans. Elsewhere in this book are examples of more recent serious artists (Betsabeé Romero, Livio De Marchi, Jose Benavides, Rebecca Caldwell, and Rubén Ortiz-Torres) for whom the car is an artistic platform.

For Blank, the definition of what makes a car an art car is complex. "An art car," Blank says, "is often a fantasy made into reality, a symbol of freedom, and a rebellious creation. Not only does an art car question the standards of the automobile industry, it expresses the ideas, values, and dreams of an individual. There are no rules for making one, and no boundaries or guidelines to follow. Art cars are therefore different from custom cars, lowriders, monster trucks, step vans, historical vehicles, and racecars, because all of those classifications have rather strict definitions. While people who create these other types of vehicles aim to embellish, enhance, and/or customize the inherent beauty and power of a given automobile, art car artists strip this away, making completely different creations."

A great many art car creators use their vehicles on a regular, even daily basis. Some of the cars are quite outrageous; you have to wonder how the public reacts when confronted with a Checker limousine that's been covered in synthetic fur, or a Dodge Aspen with an outer layer of Pez dispensers, to cite two actual examples. "The average person doesn't even think about pressures to conform until he or she confronts those forces by driving an art car," Blank says. "To me, the very medium of art cars is a form of rebellion, an act of bravery, and simply revolutionary."

Most people probably would admit that they don't know much about art cars. But they do know what they like, and for most of them it's definitely two thumbs up.

For Harrod Blank, of course, the issue was never in doubt. "One of the hottest art forms of the millennium," Blank says, "art cars juxtapose contemporary self-expression with an unexpected canvas, the almighty icon of the automobile." ☉

THE GUITCYCLE: Ray Nelson has two passions in life: guitar music and motorcycles. In fact, back in the 1970s he was known as the number one singer of motorcycle songs. Nelson, who lives in San Jose, California, is still making music. He has found an unusual way to combine the things he loves most: It's called the Guitcycle, pictured above.

This unique vehicle, which is capable of going 100 miles per hour, is built on a 1980 Yamaha 650cc motorcycle and features a sound system that plays his favorite guitar music. The body of the guitar is constructed of fiberglass, two large sheets of plywood, and 100 pounds of plaster.

Since its completion in 1981, Ray has put well over sixty-thousand miles on the Guitcycle, including coast-to-coast rides across Monster Nation to promote his band and his nonprofit charity Guitars Not Guns, which was set up to put guitars into the hands of needy children. Not being the sort of guy to simply sit on his laurels, or his Guitcycle for that matter, Ray is now at work on his new project, Acousticar. Stay tuned.

MONSTER ART CARS

DAVID CROW

You ought to drive a mile in this man's shoe

David Crow's Red Stiletto three-wheeled motor vehicle was the indirect result of an argument he once had with his girlfriend. The matter in question was her purchase of a pair of shoes—well, make that three pairs. On further reflection he realized that her love of shoes was not that much different from the way he and his fellow hot rodders felt about cars; they positively lusted after them. "The more I thought about it," Crow says, "I realized my fetish for cars was very like her fetish for shoes. Then the idea just hit me: Wouldn't it be cool to combine the two images and make a motorized stiletto?"

Built from scratch, the Red Stiletto has a 1972 Honda CB-350 motorcycle engine and running gear and a chassis composed of alloy tubing. The body, which is to say the shoe, is molded fiberglass. Crow considers the completed trike a combination of art car and custom car.

Debuted in 1997, Red Stiletto won the 1998 prize for Best Art Car in the Houston Art Car Parade. Red Stiletto has attracted admiring crowds from the first day that it appeared, so much so, in fact, that it has caught Crow by surprise. "I was not anticipating such public response to the image," he reports, "but some people feel I have achieved my goal: to make the sexiest car ever." The idea appears to have some traction: At least one major automaker has developed a concept car with two front wheels and one rear wheel, with an elevated rear end. ◉

MONSTER ART CARS
BETSABEÉ ROMERO

Betsabeé Romero's *Velvet, Acrylic, and Oil on Buick, East Los Angeles 2001.*

Internationally known Mexican artist Betsabeé Romero is fascinated with cars. In recent years she has concentrated on the automobile in a host of different ways. On a smaller scale, she creates artistic renderings of auto parts, such as tires, hubcaps, and rearview mirrors, made from native Mexican clays and glazed in bright colors. On a larger scale, she covers or fills cars with unexpected materials, such as muffins, velvet, and roses.

Trained in Mexico and France in communication, marketing, and semiotics, as well as in Pre-Columbian and Western art history, Romero brings a unique vision to the world of art cars. "In the streets, among people who work with cars," she says, "I found a closely knit community with their

art projects into their world. Here, in addition to restoring old wrecks, they also keep alive memories and give meaning to these damaged cars. They were curious about what I was doing and observed carefully. They listened and provided fresh interpretations of the work. They gave me many good ideas and offered all kinds of help. And, with great generosity they housed these art projects where they live and work."

"Copying their traditional techniques," she continues, "I wanted to draw a clear line between this process and the industrial production of cars." Art critics have said that Romero's work is an homage to, and extension of, the artistry of lowrider culture, in which factory-made objects are enhanced

JOSE BENAVIDES

Jose Benavides, at 54, has been making art for 30 years. With a masters degree in fine arts and a bachelor of science degree in mechanical engineering, he has the right set of credentials for making art cars. "I started out as a folk artist," the Arizona resident says, "and now [a number of years later] with my masters [degree] I've returned to the folk art genre. I'm trying to bring together the idea of the car, the culture of the car, and the way American design is used to accommodate the car—not just roads and garages but the way buildings are designed to accommodate the automobile."

Madonna, pictured at right, is a recent Benavides contribution to the art car genre. It is constructed on the frame of a 1979 Datsun pickup truck. The body of this motorized sculpture is composed of more than five hundred license plates held in place with 3,600 rivets. For Benavides, the license plate holds a special significance.

"License plates are legal documents, unique. Each plate," Benavides says, "represents an individual or a family or a couple that might have driven their car to Disneyland, might have had a flat, they could have had a baby in it, gone cross country, gotten lost—just a whole history. I don't know what the history is, but it is represented in that license plate. So putting all these license plates together, it's like a history book of ordinary people in America."

The reception afforded Madonna over the past couple of years has inspired Benavides to begin work on more art cars. One of these new works, commemorating the farm laborers advocate Cesar Chavez, is based around a larger-than-life tractor.

As for Madonna, Benavides will continue to show the work in art car parades and festivals around the country. Given its size and shape, driving the vehicle is not all that simple to accomplish. "The steering wheel," he says, "is inside the metal part where the rearview mirrors are. There are a couple of holes to stick your hands in, and the steering wheel is in there. The seat is set right on the rear axle, so it's kind of a rough ride. It's not street legal, but I can drive it in parades." ◉

Jose Benavides at the wheel of his inspired creation.

MONSTER
ART CARS
FRED KANTER

Art cars.
Boat cars.
Concept cars.
The ABCs of
Fred Kanter's world.

Question: How best to describe someone who owns a classic car collection, a large automotive aftermarket supply company, a trucking company that specializes in transporting exotic cars, and a state-of-the-art manufacturing facility that creates concept vehicles for major manufacturers—and who drives around town wearing bright floral Hawaiian shirts in a car that looks like a motorboat? Answer: Fred Kanter.

According to Kanter, his love of all things automotive began at an early age. "When I was born," he says, "my father drove me home from the hospital in a maroon 1941 Oldsmobile 6-cylinder, 4-door sedan. That was in 1945, and I'm sure that's what got me started."

Kanter's aftermarket business began in 1960 when he, his brother Dan, and another friend bought an old Packard for fifty dollars. "It needed an engine and some fixing," Kanter recalls. "There were a lot of spare parts in the back seat and in the trunk that didn't belong to the car. So after we fixed the car up we sold the excess parts to other collectors for more than we'd paid for the car. That's when the idea was born that hey, you can have your car and your money too. We then went out and bought more parts from Packard dealers, who

> **" After we fixed the car up we sold the excess parts to other collectors for more than we'd paid for the car. "**

were going out of business at that time. We sold them through auto flea markets and through the mail and it became a business, one that ultimately supported our habit of collecting antique automobiles. In the beginning Packard was one hundred percent of our business, but it's now only about four percent, the rest being mechanical replacement parts for American cars from the 1930s up to the 1980s. Even with that, we're now selling more dollars in Packard parts than we ever have. We carry the full dealer stock of Packard parts; everything from a frame to a clock-winding knob."

By the late 1990s Kanter had amassed a collection of Packards and other antique and classic cars, including some unusual vehicles like a Chrysler Airflow, two Muntz Jets, and numerous one-off concept cars and manufacturers' prototypes. It was around this time that he discovered what really unusual vehicles looked like. "An artist friend of mine told me about the art car parade in Houston. I went down there, met Harrod Blank (see page 118), and it was just a hoot—more fun than I had ever had in my life. I knew I had to do this. The first one I made was an eight-door Checker Airport Limousine done up as a

When Fred Kanter promised to take his wife on a cruise to celebrate their marriage, this boat was not exactly what she had in mind.

noodle car. We painted my son's name on the side and fastened an old office chair on the trunk, and he sat on it with a seatbelt that said 'King of Noodles.' His crown was a kitchen colander. The Checker towed a Subaru done up with brown foam and red paint. That was the meatball. It was followed, quite logically, by an International Harvester high-top ambulance in brilliant pink and white with Pepto Bismol bottles glued all over it."

It was at another art car event in Houston that Kanter discovered the joys of boating on dry land. After driving Matt Slimmer's Toyboata in the art car parade, he built a boat car for his wife, calling it Cruising Together. One thing led to another, and he is now completing work on his fourth boat car. The vehicles are constructed on a

> ❝ I was also interested in building replicas of 1950s concept cars, many of which no longer exist. ❞

variety of small- to medium-size front-wheel-drive chassis, like Toyota's or the Pontiac Grand Am. He calls himself the world's only art car manufacturer, complete with the *nom de vehicle* "Henry Fraud." "People go wild," he says, "when they see our boat car, and ask where they can buy one. There's a real market for them."

The boat cars are built in the shops of his latest venture, Kanter Concepts, in Santa Ana, California. "I was also interested in building replicas of 1950s concept cars, many of which no longer exist," Kanter reports. "I have a lot of collector friends who want these types of cars and they can't buy them because a museum, or the manufacturer, still owns them, if they exist at all. I went around trying to find companies capable of building such vehicles

A FRED KANTER CONCEPT CAR

Fred Kanter's first factory-concept vehicle, the Hyundai HCD 8 (pictured here), debuted at the 2004 Detroit Auto Show to wide acclaim. He now has concepting offers from other manufacturers, including one of the big three American automakers. "One reason I got into the concept car business," he says, "is because I wanted to have an influence on what Detroit produces. I think that Detroit has lost some of its magic; I think the public has realized that because the market share of American cars here is hovering around fifty percent. Fifty years ago it was virtually one hundred percent. At this point, we're building concept cars that the manufacturers design. What we hope to do is come up with original designs and sell those to the major automakers. I want to affect the American automobile industry—with cars that have a sense of color and of design excitement."

and found one that was going to be shut down by a major corporation. So I bought the company, with the idea of building concept cars for the original-equipment manufacturers and then using any down time we had to build the replicas and art cars for sale. We have already completed several builds for car companies and one boat car, in addition to our other projects in the aerospace, military, and architectural fields. We are also working with a number of prominent sculptors on their art commissions."

"We have a five-axis mill," Kanter continues, "which has a bed that is 28 feet long, 11 feet wide, and eight feet high. We can mill anything that big, whether it be a car or a sculpture."

For Kanter, the elegant cars of years gone by had a racy appeal that is rooted in the human form. "In the history of cars that have been phenomenally successful and have stood the test of time in design criteria," Kanter says, "they are often the cars that mimic the human body. The XK 120 Jaguar, the Packard Darrin, the French Delahayes and Delages, and even the early Corvettes had an appealing wasp waist: In the middle of the car, it's pinched. The doors are cut down or the body gets narrower and the rear fenders bulge out, and that's the waist of the car, and then there are the prominent, curvaceous front fenders."

Some people might think it improbable that a guy who wears Hawaiian shirts, drives down the road in a boat, and thinks cars are sexy can hope to change the look of the American automobile, but then they probably don't know Fred. ◉

MONSTER ART CARS

LISA NIGRO

Does your town have public transportation like this?

When the Monster Garage series took its first extended look beyond the Long Beach confines of Monster Garage, in a Fall 2003 special called *American Monsters*, one of the most memorable vehicles bore the name Draka. The fact that Draka is a fire-breathing beast is just one of many characteristics that made it stand out in that television special. Bearing the full name Draka, The Flaming Metal Dragon, the scaly Monster is 124 feet long, 12 feet wide, and 22 feet high. It has dinosaurian wings that span out to 30 feet. It's a creature, and a vehicle, that is surely worthy of that much-overused word *awesome*.

Draka is the creation of San Francisco artist and metal sculptor Lisa Nigro. According to Nigro, Draka was inspired by the ancient Chinese spiritual dragon Shen Lung, who controls the wind and rain. Nigro built Draka as an art installation for the Burning Man festival, held annually in the Nevada desert (and a great place to see creatively designed and modified Monster vehicles). In addition to being a work of metal sculpture, Draka also serves, in Nigro's words, as a "party wagon extraordinaire" and, during Burning Man, as "public transportation"–truly a multipurpose vehicle in the Monster Garage spirit.

Draka's front section is built on a 1980 Ford Econoline one-ton truck. The rest of the articulated body consists of three connected trailers. Behind the trailers is a long reptilian tail that swooshes back and forth. Scales on all the sections were cut from 55-gallon barrels, painted, and welded into place.

The fire-breathing Draka at night.

Draka's first trailer section consists of a kitchen, a bar, and a lounge with curved red velvet benches and a zebra print rug. The second trailer, dubbed the "entertainment car," carries musicians, a DJ, and other performers. The final trailer holds maintenance supplies and a generator. Beside the driver's seat in the front cockpit is a second seat for the designated "flame-thrower controller," whose job it is to release propane from a 30-gallon tank, and send the gas solenoid valve to an ignition device situated in the dragon's throat. With the flip of a switch, a thunderous burst of flame 25 feet long spews out into the darkness. ⚙

MONSTER ART CARS
LIVIO DE MARCHI

Jaguars, Benzes, and Bugs that float

Livio De Marchi was born in Venice, Italy, where he began his training as a sculptor in the Venetian tradition of apprenticeship in the workshop of a local craftsman. He also studied art at the Accademia di Belle Arti, where his skill in working with a variety of materials, including marble, bronze, and wood, was quickly recognized. Ultimately it was wood that fascinated and inspired him to the point where he began to work with it almost exclusively. It has, as he puts it, "a vitality which other materials do not."

After becoming well known as a sculptor of such everyday objects as coats, hats, shoes, and books, as well as of other more abstract works, he had an experience that added yet another dimension to his art. While rowing through the canals of Venice one day in 1988, he was overwhelmed by the sheer volume of traffic he encountered. His response was to create the first of his floating automobiles, a 1937 Jaguar, sculpted of wood entirely by hand, and then motorized.

Eventually the Jaguar was followed by a Fiat Topolino, a Volkswagen Beetle convertible, a gull-wing Mercedes 300SL, and a Ferrari F50. All of the sculptures are life-size, and each has a motor.

The famous humorist and *New Yorker* magazine writer Robert Benchley, on arrival in Venice, is said to have cabled his editors in New York, "Wonderful city. Streets flooded—please advise." In more recent years in Venice, it is not uncommon to see Livio De Marchi motoring about the canals among the gondolas and the delivery boats. Perhaps De Marchi should be credited with some major Monster ingenuity: He's figured out how to drive a car on those flooded streets. ⚙

MONSTER ART CARS

REBECCA CALDWELL

Not many Gothic cathedrals started out as a '71 Caddy hearse

Rebecca Caldwell traces her beginnings as an art car devotee to the late 1980s. One day that year, while riding in the San Francisco area in a Datsun that she and her boyfriend had customized with some personal touches—including a toy-dinosaur hood ornament—she spied Harrod Blank's Camera Van on the street (see page 118). "We sped up and got close to it," Caldwell recalls, "and I was just blown away. I'd never seen anything like it, and I thought, 'He's taken it all the way.' It opened a door in my imagination. So when the Datsun died, I said, 'We're going to do another art car, and this time I want to go all the way.'"

Caldwell next proceeded to build two art cars: a Honda covered with computer circuit boards and dinosaurs, and a haunted house–themed Volvo station wagon. Then she began work on what has become one of the most famous art cars on the road. Its name is Carthedral.

"I bought this hearse in 1995," she says, "and it was really clean, immaculate. I knew that I would change it into an art car, but I really wanted to know what I was doing— not just haphazardly gluing stuff to it. So I let it stew from then until 1999. The Volvo was dead by then, so the timing was perfect. And one day it hit me. I had been going to Burning Man and to art car festivals, and I had been inspired by all that creativity around me; I just knew I really wanted to go over the top. So that's when I decided to put another car on top of the hearse. I started doing sketches of the hearse with all the different elements I wanted on it, and I started seeing a cathedral— very gothic—and that was it. I would put these gothic architectural elements on it and make it a Carthedral."

As she worked on Carthedral over the next four years, Caldwell taught herself how to weld, to use an acetylene torch, to work with fiberglass, to make mosaics—whatever it took to turn her vision into reality. "Even when I wasn't physically working on it with my hands, I was mentally working on it," she remembers. "I would stare at it, and stare at the drawings. I'm a painter, so I looked at it like I was composing a painting—looking at the lines and how they were in relationship to other lines. I was using all I had learned as an artist and craftsperson to make it. I always took my painting very seriously. Unfortunately, when you get too serious about something it tightens you up, so working on an art car in a medium that isn't my normal medium loosens me up—releases a creative spirit that allows anything to happen. Another thing is that there's such a history with painting, but with art cars I really feel like we're creating our own language and our own aesthetic, and creating our own world with it. So that also frees me up. I've learned that you've got to play in order to really give something to life."

It was in 1996, well before work had commenced on Carthedral, that Caldwell made her first trip to the Burning Man festival. "I was so amazed by the people and what they had created that I instantly knew I had found my tribe. I was inspired to create something unique to contribute to the landscape and the collective experience. The following year I brought my first art car, the Honda, there. I met the greatest people and had so much fun with it that in 1998 I built my second art car, the flat-black, haunted house–inspired Volvo— a precursor to Carthedral. By then I had met dozens of other art car creators, including Harrod Blank, David Best, and Rockette Bob, and their work heavily influenced the conception of Carthedral."

The finished vehicle, which has enough interior space to stand in, is fully self-contained with a propane stove, refrigerator, double bed, and toilet. It made its debut at Burning Man in 2000 and is now an annual fixture at the event. "It might sound trite or clichéd to say that Burning Man changed my life," Caldwell reports, "but it's true." ◉

MONSTER TOUCH

EVEN A MONSTER WANTS TO LOOK GOOD—WHAT
MONSTER MAKERS DO TO GIVE THEIR RIDES THE RIGHT LOOK

MONSTER TOUCH

CUSTOMIZE

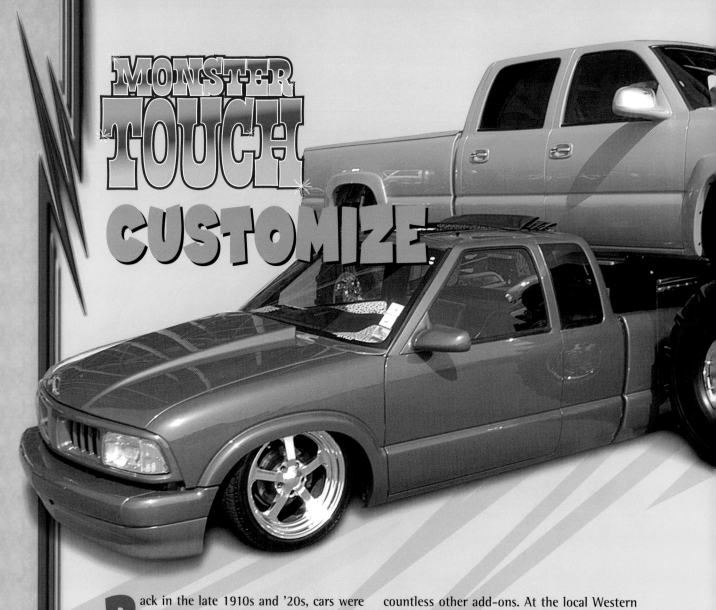

Back in the late 1910s and '20s, cars were becoming commonplace. Simply owning one was, in itself, no longer enough to stand out from the crowd. Owners who felt lost in the small crowd started searching for ways to personalize their machines. An industry sprang from their desire to be different.

The Model T Ford alone supported a huge accessory business. The bare, unadorned car that came off Ford assembly lines was the automotive equivalent of a blank canvas in front of an artist. An owner could send away to Sears for hood and fender antirattle springs, a circulating water pump, a Boyce Motometer temperature gauge plus a winged radiator cap to mount it on, seat covers trimmed with Spanish-grain leatherette, rubber pedal pads, a foot-pedal accelerator, and

> CUSTOMIZING IS ALMOST AS OLD AS THE AUTOMOBILE ITSELF. THERE'S AN HONORABLE TRADITION IN NOT LEAVING WELL ENOUGH ALONE.

countless other add-ons. At the local Western Auto store, a young rake bent on making his car speak for him could pick up a vacuum engine whistle that, with proper technique, would deliver a shrill wolf whistle. A Model T owner seeking speed could buy an overhead-valve Rajo or Roof cylinder head (the Roof was one of several 16-valve heads made for Model Ts), a Winfield carburetor, an Atwater Kent distributor ignition system, and many other hop-up parts. The Model T engine remained a favorite of both track racers and street racers well into the 1930s because so much speed equipment was available for it. Mechanically inclined owners tinkered endlessly to make their Ts look and perform the way they wanted, often spending more than the cost of the car on modifications. Just like today.

Prewar speed merchants had been based in the industrial midwest and east, but many of the outfits that would become the biggest names in specialty automotive parts set up shop in sunny California after World War II. Hot rodding and customizing came to be seen largely as California phenomena through the 1950s and 1960s, although customizers and hop-up artists were everywhere in America. Nonetheless, a never-fail marketing tactic for almost any new custom-car part in the middle of the 20th century was to bill it as "the latest California craze!" and then just sit back and watch the bucks roll in. Making a car look and perform the way you want is easier today than ever before, thanks to the ever-growing industry that sprang from those roots.

Styles, technology, and methods have changed, but today's speed and custom tricks still follow the patterns set by the pioneers. So don't worry when you start to think about doing something different to your car; it's part of your heritage.

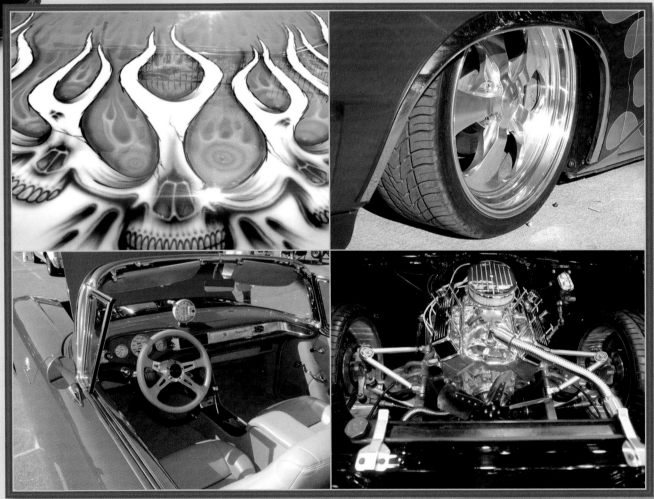

Bold, imaginative paint, radical lowering and billet wheels, high-quality engine and chassis craftsmanship, and custom interiors—all are among the things you routinely see on the streets of Monster Nation. You don't have to go all out to give a car or truck the Monster Touch. You may start with simple changes, such as a set of custom wheels, paint or vinyl graphics, and some bolt-on body mods.

MONSTER TOUCH PAINT

Paint is the surest route to a standout pride. Whether it's a brilliant candy color that looks elbow-deep and sticky-sweet, trendy pastel graphics and splashes, a rich base color with surrealistic airbrushed fantasies, or fierce multicolor flames over basic black, a great paint job has the power to draw admirers from across the show field or across the street.

Custom car painting has drawn from many fields to become an art form in itself. Pinstriping, decoration found on the carriages and cars of the rich and royal (and on pottery and other art objects for centuries before that), was taken up by custom painters in the 1950s. Stripers such as Von Dutch and Tommy the Greek painted the traditional thin lines to accent character lines and contours on the car body, but then went farther by creating elaborate, intricate decorations that became styling features in themselves. Outlined gold striping that delineated panels on fire engines and circus wagons found its way into the

hot rod painting repertoire, as did sign painters' lettering and graphic techniques. Scallops that suggested speed and streamlining on airplanes and racecars of the 1930s showed up on 1950s customs. Then painter Larry Watson took scallops even farther and covered entire cars in elaborate paint trails that flowed over and around every panel. Flames sprang from scallops; both disappeared for a while, but flames have come roaring back. Scallops live on now as tribal graphics and other wildly wandering designs.

Custom painters also experimented with the paint itself. Candy colors—translucent color coats over a reflective gold, silver, copper, or pearl-white base; metal-flake—a reflective paint

Upper left: A 350Z takes on a mammal's—or perhaps fish's—aura with black stripes over orange paint. Upper right: This Caddy sports a teardrop-style flame design. Lower left: Black flames look almost like cutouts in the red truck hood, continuing the theme set by the cutouts in the custom grille. Lower right: Bold shockwaves accent a striking two-tone treatment.

base containing, yes, flakes of metal; and pearlescent colors are just some of the finishes pioneered by imaginative custom painters. At the other end of the spectrum were builders who shot the bodywork with dark grey primer and left it at that. The black suede-looking finish was common on street rods, often intended to imply that looks didn't matter—the whole budget went into go-fast gear. Today the suede look is popular with nostalgia rodders, among others. But it's often more-durable black enamel that's been deglossed rather than primer.

Many modern base-coat/clear-coat factory finishes have the depth and shimmer available only from a custom painter not so long ago. So custom painting on newer cars often focuses on decorating the factory paint job. Pinstriping remains popular, as do flames. Bold graphic swoops, splashes, and spears add excitement to any car. And much of that decoration can be added without any paint at all. Vinyl decals and magnetic stick-ons will flame a car without using a drop of extra paint. Graphics and pinstriping decals range from subtle to audacious, and they are easily applied.

AN ART THAT KNOWS NO BOUNDS, CUSTOM PAINTING CAN BE SUBTLE OR SPLASHY. EITHER WAY, IT'S SURE TO GET A RIDE NOTICED.

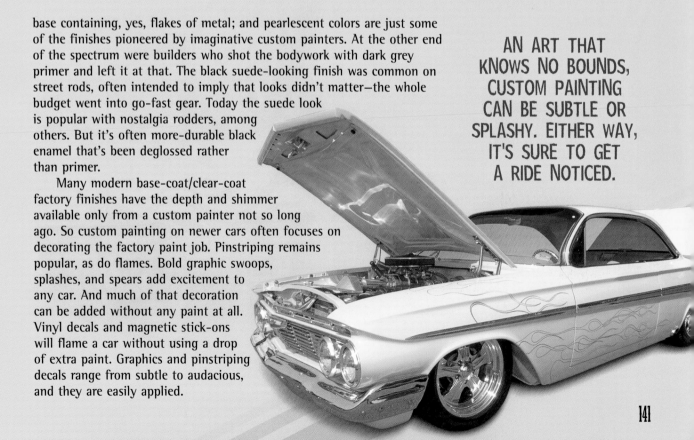

MONSTER TOUCH WHEELS

Really big wheels give a car a lighthearted, cartoony look.

One of the easiest custom touches that can be added to any car is a new set of wheels and tires. Wheels are often the first thing a car owner changes; sometimes the only thing. The extraordinary range of custom wheels available means that there is almost certainly some wheel to fit anyone's taste.

Probably the most popular look now is the large-diameter wheel—18, 20, even 22 inches in diameter—with a wide, low-profile tire. This setup, although not necessarily selected for high-performance capability, stems from racing practice where large-diameter wheels are necessary to make room for large brakes and allow air circulation to keep the hard-working brakes cool. Low-profile tires, often with sidewall height only 35 percent of tire width, keep overall outside diameter within a reasonable range and increase sidewall rigidity for crisper handling.

The now-common cast-alloy spoked wheel itself is a descendant of racing technology from

BOLTING ON A SET OF CUSTOM WHEELS IS QUICK AND EASY—IT'S THE FIRST STEP FOR A LOT OF CUSTOMS.

fifty and more years ago. Racecar designers favor lighter wheels because they help improve handling by reducing unsprung weight—the weight of the wheels, tires, brakes, and suspension parts that move with the wheels instead of being insulated from bumps by the springs. Because some early lightweight wheels were made from magnesium alloy, all cast-alloy wheels came to be called magnesium—or mag—wheels. Aluminum alloy is the material of choice now. High-style, high-price billet wheels are machined from solid chunks—billets—of aluminum, rather than being cast. Wheels are often plated, painted, or clear-coated to prevent tarnishing.

The fashionable big wheels aren't the only way to go. Nostalgia street rods in the style of the 1950s and 1960s look great—perhaps even best—on painted steel wheels with small hubcaps and trim rings. It's a look that works for a lot of muscle cars, classic pickups, and '60s restomods, too. Really nostalgic rods ride on wire wheels reminiscent of those on 1935 Fords, but with wider rims for modern tires.

Monster Nation modifiers and customizers keep their wheels and tires clean and shiny for the ultimate effect. They wash the wheels often to keep road grime and brake dust from building up and staining the wheels. A sponge or soft brush, instead of abrasive pads or wire brushes, works best. Spray-on tire dressings also keep tires from looking gray and cruddy.

MONSTER TOUCH

BODY BUILDING

From simple trim removal to complete restyling, custom bodywork makes the most radical change in how a car looks. It can also make the biggest change in the car owner's bank balance.

For quick and easy customizing, bolt-ons like grilles, headlight covers, taillight lenses, and other accessories can give a car new character. Wings, spoilers, ground-effect kits, valences and fascias, scoops, and other styling features that would otherwise have to be custom built are available ready-made. The term "bolt-on" doesn't always cover the full extent of work necessary to get the pieces onto a car and looking right, however. That

sometimes calls for bonding and molding the parts to the body and repainting the area.

The extreme case of bolt-on customizing is the kit car, where the original body, or most of it, is completely replaced by new bodywork. And some customizers place an older body, such as a 1949 Mercury, on a later chassis so they can have improved chassis and drivetrain engineering and modern ride comfort along with vintage styling.

Radical customizing or restyling calls for classic customizing techniques using metal or fiberglass. Many jobs call for professional-level skills as well as a well-equipped shop. Fabricating a new grille opening using only

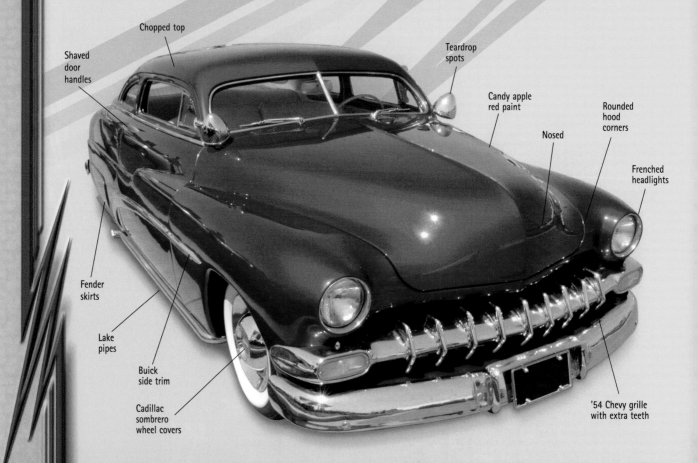

Chopped top

Shaved door handles

Teardrop spots

Candy apple red paint

Nosed

Rounded hood corners

Frenched headlights

Fender skirts

Lake pipes

Buick side trim

Cadillac sombrero wheel covers

'54 Chevy grille with extra teeth

Upper left: Smoothed seams, a top chop, and other metalwork give this 1937 Ford a smooth look. Lower left: Bodywork on the step-down Hudson includes trim removal, frenched headlights, and a custom grille opening. Upper and lower right: Bolt-on front valences give a new look without extensive custom bodywork.

sheet metal and tubing, for instance, demands advanced metalworking skills as well as a pretty good sense of style and design. Nonetheless, some of the slickest custom bodywork on the streets and in shows has been done by amateurs. Here are the basic bodywork maneuvers of Monster Nation:

Channeling: Lowering the body over the frame. Done on cars and trucks with separate body and frame. The job involves cutting the floor out of the body, setting the body down over the frame, and reattaching the floor to the repositioned body.

Chopping: Reducing the height of the top by cutting sections out of the windshield and window posts. A major job even on older bodies with flat-glass windshield and windows, top-chopping is even trickier on cars with curved windshield and window glass. Because most cars are more like pyramids than boxes above the beltline, the posts don't always want to match up after they're cut, which calls for a lot of metal massaging.

Frenching: Molding and filling seams to create a continuous contour. Frenched headlights and

> FROM BOLT-ONS TO EXTREME METALWORK, RESTYLING IS THE ULTIMATE CUSTOM TOUCH.

taillights were a common custom touch on older cars that had had removable headlight and taillight rims. Molding the rims into the body and painting them made the car look smoother and longer.

Nosing, decking, dechroming: Removing chrome ornaments from the hood, trunk lid, and sides. After the trim is pulled off, the holes for the attaching clips and studs have to be filled and smoothed. Shaving off door handles and installing solenoids to operate the latches is an old favorite custom trick. Trim removal always involves painting—at least spot painting. Factory stylists, taking a cue from customizers, now leave off a lot of the stuff that used to be removed. They've even made door handles flush.

Sectioning: Reducing the height of the body by removing a horizontal strip of metal. A complex job on slab-sided bodies, sectioning becomes downright difficult on cars with sculptured styling. Factory styling has come to reflect the proportions customizers once sought by sectioning cars, so radical bodywork like this isn't needed on late models.

MONSTER TOUCH
MAKE IT YOURS

When you customize your car, you have to follow two ironclad rules: Do things the way you want, and Do your best work.

Before you start, have a plan in mind and decide what suits you best. Would you rather spend your money on performance-enhancing parts to put under the hood and under the car or on appearance? Maybe some of each? Whatever you want is fine, but be sure you'll be happy with the results. Don't be too eager to do things just because others are doing them.

Are you customizing the car you rely on to get to work or school every day? If so, you may not be able to live with it out of commission for long periods of time to do major engine mods or bodywork. On the other hand, you can probably tie it up over a weekend without much inconvenience. And

with some preparation, you can accomplish much over a weekend. You can probably install valences and body kits, lowering kits, suspension braces, intake systems, exhaust systems, and countless other bolt-on appearance and performance items in a day or two. And often you can spread a larger project over several weekends, keeping the car driveable between work sessions. Remember, driving a work in progress is perfectly all right on the streets of Monster Nation; some even see it as a badge of honor.

For fun—and valuable support and advice for your project—hook up with a car club; clubs and Internet groups are around for virtually any automotive interest. To meet up with other people who like to fool around with cars, you can hang out at local cruise nights and go to auto swap meets, car shows, and racing events in your vicinity.

When in doubt, go wild. This Li'l Daddy Roth update on Big Daddy's Mysterion makes maximum use of paint, chrome, and hand-built panels to become a rolling sculpture. If you don't want to go quite so far, start with wheels and bolt-on parts. When it comes to looks, paint grabs the most eyeballs per buck these days. If you want to look fast and be fast, stuff a big blown engine into a small car like the Willys coupe, upper right below.

MONSTER TOUCH

SPEAKING MONSTER

IN MONSTER NATION,
THERE'S NO SUCH THING AS TOO
MANY MONSTER TOUCHES. YOU DECIDE
WHAT'S RIGHT ON YOUR CAR.

BIG BLOCK A physically large engine, such as the 454-cubic-inch Chevrolet or 429/460-cubic-inch Ford. Conversely, a small-block engine is smaller and lighter, such as the 350-cubic-inch Chevrolet or 302-cubic-inch Ford. Displacement alone isn't always a good indicator: Some small-blocks exceed 400 CID.

BIG BLOCK

BILLET A chunk of metal. In Monster Nation, the metal is aluminum and the term refers to wheels and other parts and accessories machined from solid chunks of aluminum rather than being forged or cast. Sometimes it just means an item that has been styled to look like it was machined from a billet.

BILLET

CAMMER An overhead-cam engine. Placing the cam in the cylinder head instead of the engine block lightens the valvetrain, which can improve performance. A single overhead cam (SOHC) operates both intake and exhaust valves. A double overhead cam (DOHC) has one cam for intake valves and one for exhaust valves.

CAT-BACK A performance exhaust system that replaces the pipes and muffler from the catalytic converter to the outlet. A cat-back system usually has large tubing and a free-flowing muffler.

DEUCE A 1932 Ford, not just any '30s coupe or roadster (or fiberglass replica). The coupe and roadster are famous, but there are also deuce sedans, pickups, and other body styles.

DISPLACEMENT The total volume of an engine's cylinders, stated in cubic inches (ci), cubic centimeters (cc), or liters (l). To convert metric displacement in liters to approximate cubic inches, multiply liters times 61. To convert cubic inches to approximate displacement in liters, divide cubic inches by 61. One liter equals 1,000 cc.

FLATHEAD An engine design with the valves in the engine block rather than the head. Engineers call this design, once the norm for production cars, an L-head or side-valve engine. In Monster Nation, flathead usually refers to the L-head Ford V-8

manufactured from 1932 to 1953. It was the quintessential early hot rod engine.

HEADER An exhaust manifold fabricated from tubing, designed to provide freer flow of exhaust gases than a factory exhaust manifold. Dragster headers—a separate pipe for each exhaust port—are called zoomies.

HEMI The legendary Chrysler Firepower V-8. Introduced in 1951, it had combustion chambers shaped like halves of spheres—hemispheres. Along with Dodge and DeSoto engines of similar design, it came to be known as the Hemi. Other engines before and since have had hemispherical combustion chambers, but none have been as famous for them as the Chrysler engines.

LEAD Autobody solder, used in abundance by early customizers to smooth seams and bodywork, a process called *leading*. Thus, a much-modified custom is often called a *leadsled*, even though fiberglass and plastic fillers have largely replaced lead.

LOUVERS Ventilating slots punched into a panel, such as a hood. Often they're more for looks than function.

MOUSE MOTOR

MOUSE MOTOR The legendary small-block Chevy engine.

NITRO Nitromethane, the fuel for Top Fuel class dragsters and other competition engines. Compared to gasoline, nitro doesn't burn as fast and produces less energy per pound. But because it contains oxygen that helps it burn, 1 pound of nitro needs less than 2 pounds of air for combustion while 1 pound of gasoline must be mixed with almost 15 pounds of air. A mixture with that much more fuel produces monster power. At about $35 per gallon, nitro is often used only as a fuel additive. But some racing engines run on pure nitro, consuming about a gallon per second. Drivers and crew members wear gas masks because the exhaust gases contain nitric acid vapor.

LOUVERS

NITROUS Nitrous oxide, a gas (N_2O) sprayed into an engine's intake manifold to provide extra oxygen. That oxygen, mixed with additional gasoline sprayed in at the same time, gives a monster power boost—often 100 or more additional horsepower. A shot of nitrous is somewhat like a dose of nitro for the engine. Also referred to as *juice, squeeze, the bottle, spray,* or *supercharger in a can.*

RAT MOTOR

RAT MOTOR A big-block Chevy engine.

SLAMMED A way-lowered vehicle, one that looks like it's been picked up by a giant and, yes, slammed down onto the ground. The look is also known as *in the weeds.*

SPOILER An aerodynamic device designed to disrupt airflow over a surface to prevent lift. Wings and other airfoils on cars are not for flying, but to prevent flying off the road. They improve road handling by pushing the vehicle down. Spoilers do the same by reducing lift.

SUPERCHARGER A mechanical device that forces more air-fuel mixture into the engine for increased performance. Often called a blower, it usually sits on top of the engine and is belt-driven. The classic hot rod blower is actually an exhaust-scavenging pump from a 4-71 or 6-71 GMC diesel.

T-BUCKET A hot rod with a Ford Model T roadster body, no fenders, and lots of engine. The T-bucket style started with a rod built by Norm Grabowski in the 1950s and used in the TV series *77 Sunset Strip*. The T-bucket remains popular and is easy to build because you can buy every part you need new, including the frame and a fiberglass replica body.

TUNER A late-model compact sports coupe or sedan modified for high performance. Tuners are front-wheel-drive cars with high-revving small-displacement engines that crank out the kind of performance once reserved for muscle cars. Lowered suspension, high-performance wheels and tires, more powerful brakes, and aerodynamic body modifications are usually part of the overall tuner package. Some cars have the tuner look, but without the engine modifications.

TURBOCHARGER A centrifugal supercharger driven by an exhaust-gas turbine. Turbocharger installations often include an intercooler to cool the intake charge, making it denser and increasing power.

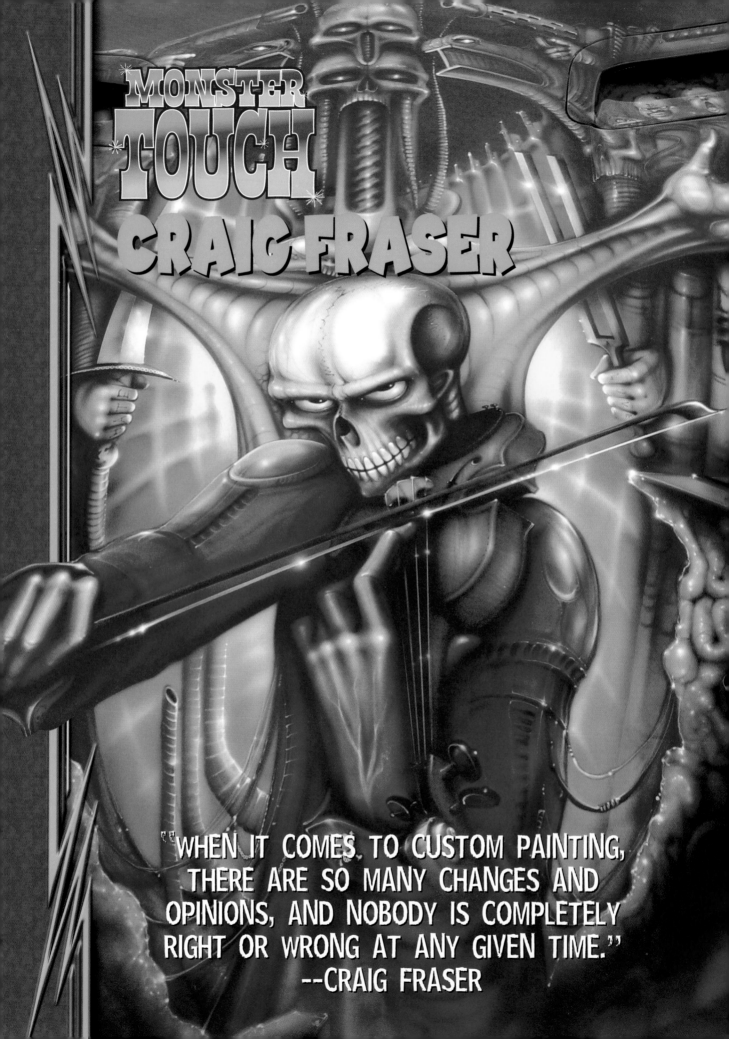

If you're looking for sizzle, paint like this is the answer. With great paint, a car or truck doesn't need very much more customizing to be a traffic-stopper.

Customizing lets a car owner make a statement, stand out from the crowd, or simply feel less like some automaker's demographic. Of all the ways to personalize a ride, a custom paint job is by far the most compelling. Aftermarket add-ons such as custom wheels, lenses, or a grille will instantly confer street cred, but they're still things that anybody with the requisite bucks can buy. A custom paint job is unique—if you do happen to see a vehicle next to you that looks exactly the same, wave to yourself; it has to be a reflection.

Thirty-eight-year-old Craig Fraser, owner and principal artist for Air Syndicate Studios at Kal Koncepts in Bakersfield, California, has been putting paint on cars and bikes for more than a decade now. His list of clients is a roll call of big car companies and notable custom car and bike builders, including West Coast Choppers, Trenz, Arlen Ness, Colorado Custom, Bones Concepts, GM, Ford, DaimlerChrysler, and House of Kolor (which is the source of paint for many of Jesse James's Monster Garage creations).

Fraser, who grew up in Bakersfield, started taking notice of things automotive at an early age.

"Growing up here you have two choices," he recalls. "You either play with horses or you play with cars, and I never did like horses too much."

Instead, he would go with his dad to the World of Wheels shows at the Civic Auditorium.

"I remember going there with my Instamatic camera when I was probably four or five, taking up rolls of film, and filling portfolios with pictures of cars," he says. This early love of cars did not

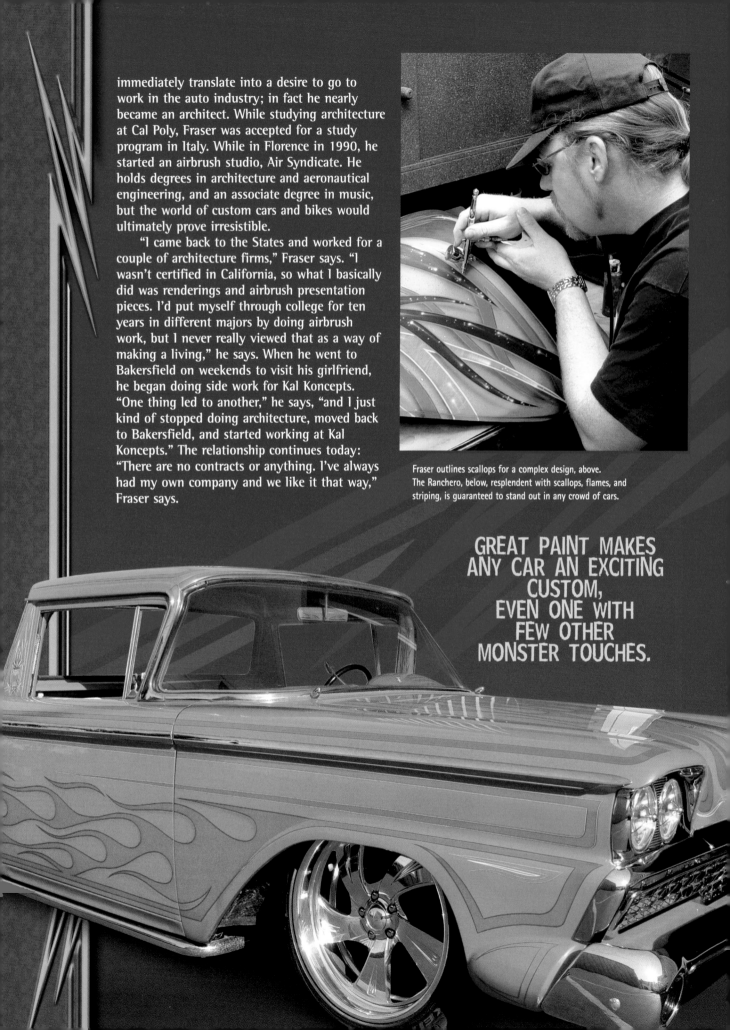

immediately translate into a desire to go to work in the auto industry; in fact he nearly became an architect. While studying architecture at Cal Poly, Fraser was accepted for a study program in Italy. While in Florence in 1990, he started an airbrush studio, Air Syndicate. He holds degrees in architecture and aeronautical engineering, and an associate degree in music, but the world of custom cars and bikes would ultimately prove irresistible.

"I came back to the States and worked for a couple of architecture firms," Fraser says. "I wasn't certified in California, so what I basically did was renderings and airbrush presentation pieces. I'd put myself through college for ten years in different majors by doing airbrush work, but I never really viewed that as a way of making a living," he says. When he went to Bakersfield on weekends to visit his girlfriend, he began doing side work for Kal Koncepts. "One thing led to another," he says, "and I just kind of stopped doing architecture, moved back to Bakersfield, and started working at Kal Koncepts." The relationship continues today: "There are no contracts or anything. I've always had my own company and we like it that way," Fraser says.

Fraser outlines scallops for a complex design, above. The Ranchero, below, resplendent with scallops, flames, and striping, is guaranteed to stand out in any crowd of cars.

GREAT PAINT MAKES ANY CAR AN EXCITING CUSTOM, EVEN ONE WITH FEW OTHER MONSTER TOUCHES.

Airbrushed fantasies, such as this war bird, can spread across whole panels, telling stories and turning a car into an exhibition of the illustrator's art.

Fraser spends about three months of each year teaching airbrush technique and custom painting in workshops throughout the country. "I teach graphics and pinstriping, although I'm sort of an unorthodox pinstriper," Fraser reports.

Developing a teaching curriculum for a field that is constantly changing is a challenge, he admits. "When it comes to custom painting, there are so many changes and opinions, and nobody is completely right or wrong at any given time," he says. "It's like fashion designers—what are they going to base the future on? It's so fickle, it follows bizarre trends." The answer, Fraser believes, is in the past. "You try to follow recurring patterns," he says. A technique or look now fashionable often "duplicates a trend that happened in the '70s in automotive customizing. Then there's color theory, which you can't get away from; it's essentially been the same since the beginning of time."

Fraser doesn't aim to teach students to paint like he does. "I really don't want to just show them a bunch of techniques and have them go off and become clones of myself," he insists. "I want them to go off and think on their own, do what I did: Take things from other industries, modify them, and use them in the automotive industry."

In addition to workshops, Fraser produces how-to videos and writes magazine columns and books on custom painting, including *Automotive Cheap Tricks and Special FX* and *Pinstriping Masters*.

"The heyday—the golden age of custom painting—wasn't in the '70s," according to Fraser. It is now. "There are more practicing custom painters in California right now" than ever before, he says. That's a bunch, because "there were more custom painters in California back then than in the rest of the world," he adds. "The custom paint industry is on such a big upswing that I don't know where it's going to end." Painting trends, Fraser believes, will evolve rather than happen in leaps. "We'll never be able to know what's going to be popular or unpopular in ten years without seeing the nine years preceding it."

He does know that car and bike painters will have to create ever-more astonishing paint jobs and won't be able to reign on reputation alone. As he puts it, "If all you want to do is sit around and hold court, you'll get what you deserve—ridicule."

"The cool thing about custom painting is that it's got a built-in governor... no one can run the show, no one's the best, and no one's the richest," he says. "This industry is like a bunch of little anarchists, and I just dig that."

So turn to the anarchists when you're wondering where to get a bunch of bang for your customizing buck. As Fraser says, "The paint job is the first thing you see, and the last thing you forget." ◉

MONSTER PLANET
THE AMPHIBIANS

Emigrating to Monster Nation: the 1951 Chevy pickup plies the waters off South Florida.

Los Carronautas

On July 16, 2003, a United States Coast Guard patrol plane spotted something unusual in the ocean about forty miles off Key West, Florida: a truck. Not some derelict piece of floating flotsam—no, this was a 1951 Chevy 3600 Series commercial flatbed truck. In fact it wasn't simply floating either, it was moving along at about eight miles per hour, propelled by its "Thrift-Master" overhead-valve, inline-six-cylinder, 92-horsepower power plant.

It is doubtful that any of the 12 Cubans aboard the vehicle had ever seen, or even heard of, Monster Garage, but the Monster Garage folks would have had respect for this crew. The men had fabricated a prow to push it through the waves, attached a propeller to its driveshaft, and kept it afloat with about a dozen empty 55-gallon metal drums.

Of all the conveyances used during the past 54 years by Cubans trying to reach Monster Nation, er, Florida, this was the most unusual. As one Coast Guardsman put it, "We've seen surfboards, pieces of Styrofoam, bathtubs, refrigerators—but never an automobile." Another remarked that it was "the most creative vessel I've seen so far."

If they had been on Monster Garage they would have gotten a set of MAC Tools for their work. But this was real life, not a TV show. The men were picked up by the Coast Guard and returned to Cuba. As for the Chevy, the Coast Guard deemed it a hazard to navigation and sent it to the ocean floor.

If that had been the end of the story it would have been incredible enough, but for two of those on that truck it was a matter of, if at first you don't succeed...

On February 4, 2004, the Coast Guard stopped yet another seagoing motor vehicle, this one a 1959 Buick carrying two veterans from the first attempt along with another eight *carronautas*, or car astronauts as they have been dubbed by their fellow Cubans.

Once again the Coast Guard, showing no regard for what the Buick would bring at a collectible-car auction, removed the passengers and sank the car. ◉

WaterCar

The March WaterCar is built on a 304-stainless-steel square-tube chassis that fits through channels fabricated into the vehicle's fiberglass body. If it looks surprisingly like a 2002 Chevy Camaro, that's because the body is an aftermarket Camaro funny-car shell. As the shell had no bottom, the car's creator, Californian Dave March, and his two sons put in about three thousand hours of trial and error perfecting the final molded version. The suspension is based on the C4 Corvette unit and the stock Corvette wheels can be raised and lowered via a hydraulic ram.

The WaterCar has a Subaru WRX engine and drivetrain mounted in the Camaro's trunk. Power is delivered via a VW Type2-style transmission on

On its lightweight stainless steel frame, the March WaterCar reaches 125 miles per hour on land and a zippy 45 miles per hour on the waves.

land and by a Berkeley jet pump on the water. The transition is made via a custom-built transfer case designed by March.

The WaterCar can be yours for $150,000. If that seems a little steep, March is planning an SUV version with a much lower sticker price. ◉

A water-powered jet propels the Aquada when the vehicle is waterborne. The jet unit itself can be steered like a rudder; the vehicle's steering wheel serves as the tiller.

Aquada

The Aquada is manufactured by Gibbs Technologies in Warwickshire, England. It hits a top speed of 110 miles an hour on land and 35 on the water. Designed by company co-owner Alan Gibbs, the three-seat vehicle utilizes the 175-horsepower, 2.5-litre Land Rover Freelander V-6 engine and a Jatco 5-speed automatic transmission. The composite body is mated to a square-tube aluminum chassis.

In the interest of maintaining a totally watertight cockpit environment, the Aquada has no doors. The rear-wheel-drive vehicle has a second axle that powers a 2,200-pound-thrust jet pump for use on the water. There is an onboard computer that monitors the transition from car to boat in order to prevent any unpleasant surprises. When the Aquada enters the water, the wheels fold up into the wheel wells; the land steering system is disabled and replaced by the unit controlling the jet pump. These, along with the other necessary mechanical changes, allow the Aquada to change from car to boat in just 12 seconds.

Gibbs, a New Zealand native, is building 100 Aquadas, and he has orders in hand for 20. ◉

LIL' MONSTERS

MONSTERS GONE MINI – WHAT THE NEXT
GENERATION OF MONSTER NATION IS DRIVING

LIL' MONSTERS
BIG RED WAGON

It's never too early to get into the Monster game. In fact, the future of Monster Nation is in the hands of kids who get the customizing bug at an early age. For 12-year-old Shane DeBerti and his 9-year-old brother, Brad, building a monster wagon was not only fun, it was part of their home-schooling curriculum. (Everyone should have a school like that.) The challenge Shane and Brad set for themselves was simple—fabricate a jammin' red wagon out of bits and pieces lying around the family garage. Of course it helped that the head of their family is Doug DeBerti (see page 30), so the stuff lying around dad's garage was far cooler than the usual collection of mismatched power tools, old garden implements, and rusty widgets. Still, dad Doug is quick to point out that the wagon was the boys' project and his role was mostly advisory.

"We first found some old quad wheels in the garage," says Doug. "Then we set out two Air Ride Technology airlift shock waves for the suspension—sort of a combination air

bag and shock absorber. We brainstormed designs for a couple of days, and Shane came up with the idea to use some tubing for the wagon body. I helped him lay out the 1-inch tubing and then he bent all the tubing for the top of the wagon. We built jack stands and put the four tires underneath the wagon bars to determine the ride height, then made cardboard templates to make a 4-link suspension using the shockwaves. They also made two sway bars to keep the wagon level. All of the bars were drilled and tapped by the boys. We then cut out two pieces of aluminum and the boys pressed in the bearings and put a plate on each side of the wheels so they would roll easily.

"I did all the welding and the boys did all of the fabricating—drilling, tapping, grinding, bending—with my guidance," he continues. "After the wagon was fully assembled and everything checked out, the boys took it apart so we could take it down to the shop and powder-coat it. Then they reassembled it."

Any doubts about why the boys went to all that trouble vanish when they see the happy smiles of the wagon's passengers. One look at Shane and Brad's big red wagon suggests that the future of our Monster Nation is in good hands. We wouldn't be surprised if Doug gave them an A+ in Monster Building 101 and followed up with a high five. Be true to your school! ✪

As the old saying goes, "It ain't work if you're having fun." Shane and Brad are obviously having tons of fun as they assemble their big red wagon. Daddy Doug did the welding and supervised the build, but the kids took care of the rest. They hauled and bent the tubing, assembled the wheels, and tweaked the suspension system. The only thing they sent it out for was a custom paint job—all the way down to dad's shop.

LIL' MONSTERS
SUPER STROLLER

As far as Aaron Wedeking, President of Premier Racing Products in Murrieta, California, is concerned, you can't start too soon when it comes to training the future generations of Monster Nation Monster makers.

"We started our stroller design using pictures of dune buggy chassis and built the frame off of those," says Wedeking. "We made custom aluminum hubs for quad wheels and tires, and to top off the suspension we used custom Sway-A-Way Racerunner shocks with piggyback reservoirs. The driver [read parent, babysitter, et al.] pushes the stroller from behind, using a MOMO steering wheel and a chain drive linked to a polished aluminum rack and pinion system. The young racer sits comfortably in PRP's Preemy Seat, held securely by DJ Safety harnesses. We added an aluminum trunk/diaper bag for the necessities. Of course all of these amenities would be useless without the Igloo ice chest/fuel cell." The total tab for this stylin' ride: about $4,000. ◉

Although it looks at first glance as if Monster, Jr., is in the driver's seat, a closer look reveals that it takes a back-seat-drivin' grown-up Monster to spin this stroller through the park.

LIL' MONSTERS
THUNDERPIG

Chuck Kaparich has an unusual job: He carves and paints wooden carousel horses. He is something of a legend in Missoula, Montana, where he created his first carousel over a four-year period beginning in 1991. The Missoula Carousel is now a top tourist attraction in the state.

What does Chuck do when he puts down his wood-sculpting tools? He picks up his auto tools and builds a neat lil' monster. Called the Thunderpig, Kaparich's unusual vehicle began life as an amusement park bumper car, a 1947 Dodgem model. He recalls, "A friend got it at an amusement park sale, and I thought, 'What a cool ride.'"

The metallic jade-green-and-flame Dodgem features frenched 1959 Caddy taillights, a custom tube chassis with a Cushman golf cart rear end, Tecumseh 4-speed tranny, centrifugal clutch, Azuza drum brakes, Moon gauges, a Sony CD player, a cherry-framed aluminum dash, and custom rolled-and-pleated upholstery in green velour and leather. ◉

HOT ROD RED WAGON

Oakland, California's Bob Castaneda is not your typical Golden State hot rodder. Bob's the guy riding around in the oversized little red wagon. While Bob's red wagon may not look like a hot rod, it's as much that as it is a little red wagon, with its tubular frame, big Chevy engine, and running gear. And how many red wagons top out at 80 miles an hour?

"I built it," Castaneda says, "as a hot rod. I'd seen a lot of art cars but I never thought about crossing over. What happened was, I had it built as a T-Bucket roadster, then changed it to this. I wanted to build something really different, and the more I thought about it, the more I liked it—so I went with it."

Constructed by Bob and his cousin, Art Baker, the project took them about a year of weekends to complete. With the addition of a removable windshield the wagon is street legal.

"Art drives it all the time as a second car," says Castaneda. "He drives it around town and has a lot of fun with it. Other than car shows I don't usually drive it, but I've had some amazing things happen when I have because everybody's got wagon stories.

"One lady told me that every Christmas she and her sister would get in their wagon and have their picture taken for that year's Christmas card. So she climbed in and we took a whole bunch of pictures for her to use as her next Christmas card. Kids love it."

Bob has plans to make the wagon a multi-theme art car, lifting the wagon off the chassis and setting alternate bodies on top.

"I've got a couple of other ideas for bodies that I'm going to build," he says. "They're all interchangeable. I have this car because I like to have fun. I'm adventurous—and, like other artists, I do it partly for the attention." ◎

Lil' Monsters

HEMI GOLF CART

What would the guys wearing blazers and drinking martinis in the clubhouse say if they saw Californian Jim Asbury, above, coming down the back nine in this contraption?

A golf cart? With its '50s-Studebaker-inspired front end and a fire-breathing, fuel-guzzling hemi sticking up into the wind, it couldn't possibly be a golf cart, right? Don't say that to Asbury. Anybody with a mind capable of thinking up something this bad-to-the-bone is not someone to be messed with.

In truth, Asbury's hemi golf cart so far is just a mock-up that he uses to scare squirrels and other small creatures. But listen up: The real thing is currently under construction, and someday soon, perhaps on your favorite golf course, this divot-digging Monster will be coming to devour your caddy—or at least your caddy's livelihood. As they say on the links: Give way! ◉

LOWRIDER LAWNMOWER

Artist Rubén Ortiz-Torres uses the Mexican-American lowrider tradition as a jumping off platform to explore aspects of modern culture. Represented in a number of prominent museums, galleries, and private collections, Ortiz-Torres works in a variety of media: painting, photography, film, video, multimedia, collage, and customized commercial products. Many of his creations feature the design motifs and technological wizardry of lowrider vehicles. He is one of Monster Nation's most serious and accomplished artists.

Among Ortiz-Torres's best-known works is Alien Toy: Unidentified Cruising Object, from 1997. Featuring a lowrider pickup truck built by world bed-dancing champion Salvador "Chava" Muñoz, the truck features 16 hydraulic systems that spin, gyrate, disassemble, and reassemble to the soundtrack of an accompanying video installation.

In 2002, Ortiz-Torres created a new lowrider-themed installation called The Garden of Earthly Delights, named after a famous 16th-century triptych by the Dutch painter Hieronymus Bosch. Ortiz-Torres's Garden features a customized tractor lawnmower, pictured above. The work has been presented to date in Los Angeles, Chicago, and Vancouver, British Columbia.

In Ortiz-Torres's words, "The Garden of Earthly Delights is a mechanical ballet where the pastoral and the industrial clash and depend on each other. The aesthetic machine is a contradictory means of expression and an end in itself. It is customized technology at the service of art, culture, and politics." The artwork is meant to provoke thought about two different strands in the lives of Southern California's Mexican-American communities. One is the role that migrant and immigrant workers have played in the tending of green spaces, such as farms and lawns. The other is the ways that machines such as cars, trucks, and lawnmowers have been both functional, job-related objects and also canvases for individuals' symbolic and artistic expression. ◉

MONSTER Shrines

EVERY NATION IS PROUD OF ITS PUBLIC MONUMENTS, AND MONSTER NATION IS NO EXCEPTION

MONSTER Shrines

CARHENGE

On Salisbury Plain in southern England stands what some have called the eighth wonder of the ancient world: Stonehenge. Attributed to everyone from Druids to aliens from outer space, Stonehenge was actually a sophisticated astronomical observatory used for more than 400 years, beginning around 1900 B.C.

On the great plains of the north central United States stands what some have called a nuisance of no use whatsoever: Carhenge. Located on U.S. 385 just north of Alliance, Nebraska, Carhenge was the brainchild of Alliance resident Jim Reinders.

Built to replicate Stonehenge, Carhenge consists of 38 cars painted a uniform shade of gray and placed in a circle approximately 96 feet in diameter. Some are buried, rear end down, in pits five feet deep, while those forming the arches have been welded into position. The "heel stone" is a 1962 Cadillac.

Built as a memorial to Reinders's father, who once lived on the farm where Carhenge now stands, it was constructed by the Reinders family and dedicated on the Summer Solstice in 1987.

Currently owned and maintained by a group called Friends of Carhenge, it has been visited by more than 80,000 tourists from all over the world. It is not known how many of them were Druids. ◉

Reports persist that on certain evenings when the moon is full, the ghost of legendary car designer Harley Earl makes a midnight appearance.

MONSTER Shrines

SPINDLE

The first time David Bermant, owner of the Cermak Plaza Mall in Berwyn, a suburb of Chicago, saw Spindle, a public sculpture he had commissioned for the mall grounds, he called it "wonderful, interesting, and provocative." Some local residents, however, took a dimmer view. "Spindle," said one, "is just more junk up our gazoos."

Created by Los Angeles–based artist Dustin Shuler in 1989, Spindle consists of eight cars impaled on a 50-foot-tall spindle. One of the cars, a 1975 BMW 2002, was owned by Bermant—who in addition to the Cermak Mall owns many others throughout the country. A supporter of the New York museum P.S.1 and a founder of the David Bermant Foundation: Color, Light, Motion, he is no stranger to controversy. The recently dismantled installation *Ghost Parking Lot,* at one of his plazas in Hamden, Connecticut, also had its share of detractors.

Shuler, an internationally acclaimed artist, bristled at the characterization of his work as "junk." "Spindle is not a stack of junk," he said. "I'm dealing with the products of our society and honoring an American icon—the automobile. To look at something everyone else looks at and yet to see it differently is the gift—some might say the curse—of the artist, and to present this unique view so that others may share this new perspective is a challenge with which artists must come to terms."

As for the complaints of some who see the sculpture as an eyesore, Shuler responds, "The French didn't want the Eiffel Tower built either." ◉

STUDEBAKER SIGN

Once upon a time two engineers, Mel Niemier and Michaek de Blimenthal, who were working for the now defunct automaker Studebaker, came up with a plan to create a giant sign unlike any other in the land—a sign so big that it would be visible only from the air. They staked out a half-mile-long sign on land that was part of the Studebaker Proving Grounds in Indiana. It was staked out because this was not a sign that was going to be erected; this sign was to be grown. In 1938 some 8,259 white pine seedlings were planted, and as they grew the Studebaker sign became a reality.

Today, some sixty-five years later, the trees, now seventy-five to eighty feet tall, are part of the Bendix Woods County Park. They are listed on the National Register of Historic Places, and the *Guinness Book of World Records* calls them the largest living advertising sign in the world.

Unfortunately the trees are beginning to show their advanced age and have suffered quite a bit from storm damage. It is not known how much longer this truly unusual automotive shrine will survive. The normal life span for these trees is only about eighty years.

If you plan to visit, the park is located on Timothy Road, south of U.S. 20, in New Carlisle, Indiana. Oh, and if you plan to actually see the word Studebaker spelled out, you'd better be driving your flying car. ◉

MONSTER Shrines

CADILLAC RANCH

n a wheat field just west of Amarillo, Texas, on Interstate 40 near the old Route 66, is one of the most famous works of public art in America: Cadillac Ranch. Ten Cadillacs buried nose down, angled into the ground at a precise 52 degrees, they stand against the skyline like some surrealist Maginot Line waiting to be assaulted by some dangerous opposition force.

Cadillac Ranch (© Ant Farm 1974) was conceived and installed by a small collective of artists known as Ant Farm. These three artists, Chip Lord, Hudson Marquez, and Doug Michels, installed the work on property belonging to Stanley Marsh III, a wealthy local art collector.

The Cadillacs, ranging from a 1949 Club Coupe to a 1963 Sedan, were purchased, driven to the site, and placed into previously excavated holes. Over the course of time the Ranch has been visited by millions of people, many of whom have taken the opportunity to place their own artistic stamps on the work in the form of graffiti. In fact, the cars are periodically repainted white in order to encourage this. The Ranch has appeared in numerous TV shows, magazine articles, and advertisements for everything from chewing gum to computers, and it was the inspiration for a Bruce Springsteen song of the same name.

As Hudson Marquez recalls, the imagery of the Cadillac had strong roots in his past: "All my childhood heroes drove Cadillacs—Fats Domino, Guitar Slim, and Yogi Berra. Studying the rear of Mr. Domino's 1957 red convertible, the cosmos snapped and revealed those reverse sloped fins as Martians with Mohawks. Exhaust grilled teeth, red-lensed eyes, and backup nostrils. Thus began my obsession with the marque.

"Seventeen years later, having discovered like-minded artists worshipping at the Tailfin Temple, the Cadillac Ranch was created. A 3-D tale of the Rise and Fall of the Tailfin." ◉

MONSTER Shrines
THE GIANT UNIROYAL TIRE

F or nearly forty years people driving into Detroit from Metro Airport on Interstate 94 have passed what is certainly one of the great automotive landmarks in this Monster Nation of ours: The Giant Uniroyal Tire. At eight tons and eight stories tall it's hard to miss.

It is doubtful that many passersby know that the tire began its life as a giant Ferris wheel at the 1964 New York World's Fair. Designed by the same architects that designed the Empire State Building, it offered rides for 25 cents and carried more than two million visitors in its 24 gondolas, including Jackie Kennedy and her two children.

When the World's Fair ended in 1965, the tire was dismantled and its 188 sections were shipped to Detroit by rail. Then the tire was reassembled over a four-month period at Uniroyal's Allen Park site.

And, just in case you were wondering, if the Monster Garage crew were to build a vehicle large enough to use the tire, it would have to be about 200 feet tall.

BIG BRUTUS

About six miles west of the junction of K7 and K102 in the town of West Mineral, Kansas, resides one of the largest self-propelled vehicles ever built: Big Brutus. If "seeing is believing" is a saying that needs any validation, Big Brutus proves the point.

Statistics alone won't prepare you for the sense of awe to be felt when you walk up to the base of the thing and crane your neck to get a glimpse of the topmost part of the shovel, looming some sixteen stories above your head.

Built over a one-year period in the early 1960s, Big Brutus required 150 railroad cars to transport all of its component parts. It weighs 11 million pounds. During its 11 years of operation it ran 24 hours a day digging up dirt at the rate of 150 tons per scoop, or enough to fill three railroad cars. One of the most amazing facts about this giant machine is that it was truly self-propelled. Four pairs of crawlers, or trucks, one at each corner of the base, moved it along at a brisk .22 miles per hour. Each pair of crawlers was powered by a 250-horsepower engine, and the gear case for each held 2,200 gallons of oil. While nobody ever claimed that Brutus was a lowrider, the big crane did stay level due to the operation of four giant 42-inch-diameter hydraulic jacks, all supplied with hydraulic fluid from a 3,200-gallon central reservoir.

Brutus was shut down in 1974 for economic reasons. The electric bill alone for its last month in operation was $27,000.

As big as Big Brutus is, there was another even larger monster crane in Cumberland, Ohio, the 13,500-ton Big Muskie. Big Muskie went to earthmover heaven in 1999, leaving Big Brutus to remind us that mechanical giants did indeed once roam the earth. ◉

Photo Credits

Page 1 left and right: Matthew Eberhart

1 center: Rick Dobbertin

10 to 17: Rick Dobbertin

20 to 27: HB Artworks, Inc.

30 to 37: Matthew Eberhart

40 and 41: Dean Jeffries Automotive Styling

42: Matthew Eberhart

44 and 45 top: Matthew Eberhart

44 bottom: Dean Jeffries Automotive Styling

45 bottom: Dean Jeffries Automotive Styling

46 and 47: Dean Jeffries Automotive Styling

50 to 52: Matthew Eberhart

53: Galpin Motors

54 to 57: Matthew Eberhart

60 and 61: Mark Langello

62 and 63 bottom: Mark Langello

64 to 66: Jerry Bowers/Shortcut High, Inc.

67 top row and lower left: Jerry Bowers/Shortcut High, Inc.

70 to 72: Matthew Eberhart

73: Wayne Harris/dB Drag Racing

74 and 75 top: Matthew Eberhart

74 and 75 center and bottom rows: Scott Owens/Pioneer

76 top row: Matthew Eberhart

76 bottom left: Scott Owens/Pioneer

76 bottom right: Wayne Harris/dB Drag Racing

77: Wayne Harris/dB Drag Racing

80 and 81: Matthew Eberhart

82 top: Steve Coonan

82 and 83 bottom: Steve Coonan

83 top: Matthew Eberhart

84 top left: Boyd Coddington

84 top right: Matthew Eberhart

84 and 85 bottom: Steve Coonan

85 top left: Steve Coonan

85 top right: Matthew Eberhart

86: John Bramley

88 to 93: Steve Coonan

94: Steve Bonge

95 upper left and bottom: Steve Bonge

95 upper right and middle row: John Bramley

96 to 102: Matthew Eberhart

103: Falken Tire

105 lower right: John Bramley

106 and 107: Matthew Eberhart

108 top and bottom: Matthew Eberhart

108 center (two): Temecula Rods & Customs

109 to 113: Matthew Eberhart

114: Franco Sbarro/Espera Sbarro

115 top: Carolinen

115 lower left: Dingo/Rinspeed

115 lower right: Rinspeed

118 and 119: Alexis Spottswood

120 to 122: Photo © Harrod Blank

123 bottom: Photo © Harrod Blank

124: Galeria Ramis Barquet

125: Photo © Harrod Blank

126: Matthew Eberhart

127 and 128 top row: Fred Kanter

128 bottom row: Matthew Eberhart

129: Hyundai Motor America

130 and 131: Lisa Nigro/Gabe Kirchheimer

131 inset: Lisa Nigro/Thomas Sepe

132 to 133: Livio De Marchi

134 to 135: Photo © Harrod Blank

138 to 149: Matthew Eberhart

150 to 153: Craig Fraser

154: Getty Images

155 top: Bob Brown

155 bottom row: Gibbs Technologies

158: Matthew Eberhart

159: Doug DeBerti

160 and 161: Matthew Eberhart

162: Dana Nichols

163: Photo © Harrod Blank

164: Matthew Eberhart

165: Ruben Ortiz-Torres

168 and 169: Michael C. Snell

170: Dustin Shuler

171: St. Joseph County (Indiana) Parks

172 and 173: Cadillac Ranch/ Ant Farm © 1974 (Lord, Marquez, Michels)

174: Uniroyal Tire

175: Michael C. Snell

All other photographs provided by Discovery Communications, Inc., and contributing photographers: Steve Bonge, John Bramley, Rahoul Ghose, Cat Gwynn, Chris Hildreth, Virginia Lee Hunter, Clint Karlsen, Daniel Lincoln, Dave Lindsay, Clay McLachlan, David McNew, Gilles Mingasson, Beatrice Neumann, Gary Payne, Rick Scherer, Peter Taylor

Additional Reading

Blank, Harrod. *Wild Wheels.* Pomegranate Artbooks, 1994.

Blank, Harrod. *Art Cars.* Lark Books, 2002.

Coddington, Boyd, and Tony Thacker, editor. *Hot Rods by Boyd.* Thaxton Press, 1997.

DeWitt, John. *Cool Cars, High Art: The Rise of Kustom Kulture.* University of Mississippi Press, 2001.

Donnelly, Nora, editor. *Customized: Art Inspired by Hot Rods, Low Riders and American Car Culture.* Abrams, 2000.

Green, George W. *Special Use Vehicles.* McFarland & Co., 2003.

Ortiz-Torres, Ruben. *Desmothernismo.* Huntington Art Center, 1998.

Romero, Betsabeé. *Body Shop* (Exhibition Catalog). Galeria Ramis Barquet, New York, 2002.

Sandoval, Denise, and Patrick A. Polk. *Arte y Estilo: The Lowriding Tradition.* Petersen Automotive Museum, 2000.

Shapiro, Harvey. *Man Against the Salt.* Minerva Press, 1997.

Silk, Gerald, et al. *Automobile and Culture.* Abrams, 1984.

Vose, Ken. *The Convertible: An Illustrated History of a Dream Machine.* Chronicle Books, 1999.

Witzel, Michael, and Kent Bash. *Cruisin': Car Culture in America.* Motorbooks, 1997.